A Year Full Of

Stories

366 Stories and Poems

Georgie Adams *and* Selina Young

Dolphin
GIANT

For
Fiona who began it…and who helped me all the
way through and Judy, for healing reflexology.
With love, G.A.

Published in paperback in 1999
First published in Great Britain in 1997
by Orion Children's Books
a division of the Orion Publishing Group Ltd
Orion House
5 Upper St Martin's Lane
London WC2H 9EA

A catalogue record for this book is available
from the British Library
Printed in Italy by Printer Trento S.r.l.

ISBN: 978-1-85881-672-2

Contents

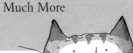

Contents

Contents

📋1 A Good Start

It was the first day of the New Year. Ben was getting dressed in his room.
"I can't find my socks," said Ben.

"They must be there somewhere," said Mum.

Ben rummaged through a heap of clothes. He found shorts, a shirt, two jumpers, a vest and . . . THERE were his socks at the bottom.

"Time to tidy up, I think," said Mum. So Ben put his socks on, and folded his clothes in a drawer. "Well done," said his mum.

Ben searched for his shoes. He found the left shoe by the bookcase, but the right shoe was missing.

"I can't find my shoe," said Ben.

"It must be there somewhere," said Dad.

It wasn't on the shoe rack, or behind the door. So Ben looked under the bed. He found a balloon, some crisps, five marbles and . . . his playful puppy, Boris. And . . . THERE was his shoe at the back.

"Time to tidy up, I think," said Dad. So Ben tied his shoelaces, and cleared everything off the floor. "Well done," said Dad.

After that Ben went to find his dumper truck. It had great big wheels and the back tipped up. But when Ben opened the toy cupboard - everything fell out.

"You'll never find your truck in that mess," said Mum.

"It must be there somewhere," said Dad.

"TIME TO TIDY UP, I THINK," said Ben. So Ben picked up his puzzles, sorted the games, and put his toys back in the cupboard. Last of all . . . . . THERE was his favourite truck.

"You've made a good start to the year," said Mum and Dad. Ben looked around his clean and tidy room.

"Yes," said Ben, "I HAVE!"

2 Little Star

Twinkle, twinkle, little star
I see you in the sky.
If I see you,
Can you see me
With your twinkling eye?

Do you wonder what I am,
Tucked up in bed at night?
Do you sleep
While I'm awake
In the morning light?

Twinkle, twinkle, little star
Shining clear and bright.
Tonight I think
I saw you wink,
As if to say, "Goodnight!"

3 The Man in the Moon

The Man in the Moon
In a hot-air balloon
Came down to see the Queen.
But the Queen was away
For a year and a day,
Riding her sewing machine.

The Man in the Moon
Went round the world
And found the Queen in Spain.
So they flew the balloon
Back up to the moon,
And never came back again.

4 The Hat and the Tum Tum Tree

One day Mr Bear was out walking, when the wind blew his nice new hat to the top of the Tum Tum tree. "Oh, bother!" said Mr Bear.

Just then Stripy Tiger came along and, seeing Mr Bear in trouble, he offered to help. "If I stood on you," said Stripy Tiger, "I could reach your hat at the top of the Tum Tum tree."

So Stripy Tiger stood on Mr Bear, but he couldn't reach the hat.

In a while Hee Haw Donkey came along and, seeing his two friends in trouble, he offered to help.

So Hee Haw Donkey stood on Stripy Tiger, and Stripy Tiger stood on Mr Bear, but he couldn't reach the hat.

After that Humpy Camel came by the Tum Tum tree and, seeing the difficulty his three friends were having, he offered to help.

So Humpy Camel stood on Hee Haw Donkey, Hee Haw Donkey stood on Stripy Tiger and Stripy Tiger stood on Mr Bear, but try as they might, they COULD NOT reach the hat.

Now at that very moment Giraffe With a Scarf came along and, seeing Mr Bear's nice new hat at the top of the Tum Tum tree, he offered to help.

BUT Giraffe With a Scarf didn't stand on anybody. He reached up with his long, long neck to the top of the Tum Tum tree and got Mr Bear's hat down . . . all by himself!

"Thank you!" said Mr Bear. Then Giraffe With a Scarf, Humpy Camel, Hee Haw Donkey, Stripy Tiger and Mr Bear all went home.

5 Noah's Park

Noah and the animals lived in Noah's Park.

One morning Noah was pegging out his washing, when the penguins Flip and Flap came along. They looked upset.

"What's the matter?" asked Noah.

"We haven't got anywhere to swim," said Flip.

"The elephants squirted all the water out of our pool," said Flap.

"Hm," said Noah, "I'll see what I can do."

Noah went inside and got a wash tub. Then he filled it with water. It made a splendid paddling pool for the penguins.

"Thank you, Noah!" said Flip.

"Now we can swim every day," said Flap. Noah smiled. Then he looked at his clothes hanging on the line. "You can use my tub every day *except* . . . washing days!" he said.

6 Lost Letters

I sent some letters to my friends,
But on the way I dropped them.
Someone must have picked them up,
And popped them in the post.

"It wasn't me," said Jenny Lee. "I was feeding Fred."

"It wasn't us," said James and Gus, "we were in the park."

"It wasn't Jack," said Mrs Black, "he was making biscuits."

"It wasn't Jill," said Mr Hill, "she was helping me."

I wrote some letters to my friends
And now I think I see.
The POSTMAN must have picked them up -
Everyone's here for tea.

THANK YOU VERY MUCH!

7 Bathtime

In goes the water,
Not too hot.
Squeeze out the bubble stuff,
In goes the lot.

In goes my whale
In goes my boat.
In go all the toys
That I can float.

Now my bath is ready
What else can there be?
I think I remember . . .
In goes ME.

8 Doctor Dog

Doctor Dog has lots of patients to see today. Nurse Kitty makes a list of everybody who comes to the surgery. "Next, please," says Doctor Dog.

Mrs Pig has come with her three little pigs. Potter Pig is crying. "Oh, dear, what's the matter?" says Doctor Dog.

"It's my tail," says Potter. "It won't curl!"

Doctor Dog examines Potter's tail. It's as straight as a ruler. Then he looks at the other two, which are twirly. Doctor Dog is puzzled. Potter is a very healthy little pig. "Eat an apple every day," he tells Potter. "It might help your tail."

Potter ate an apple every day for a week. The apples were good, but they didn't make his tail curl. So Mrs Pig took him back to the surgery.

"Hello," says Nurse Kitty. "Back again?" Potter tells her about his tail.

"I've got just the thing for you," says Nurse Kitty. She fetches her First Aid box and gives Potter - a hair curler. "Curl your tail up before you go to sleep," says Nurse Kitty. "*That* will make it better."

So Mrs Pig curled Potter's tail up for a week. And it worked. Potter's tail was as curly as a corkscrew from that day on. And he *still* eats an apple every day.

Jumpy Custard

If all the world was ice-cream
And all the seas were mustard
And all the skies were apple pies,
There wouldn't be any custard.

Which would be a pity because,

Frogs love it,
Even when it's lumpy.
They eat it hot
They eat it cold
They eat it when it's NINE DAYS OLD!
Custard makes them jumpy.

Prehistoric Pet

A little girl called Maggie
Had a mammoth, big and shaggy.
The front end of Jim
Looked grizzly and grim,
But the tail end was friendly and waggy.

Hot-Buttered Ghost

I saw a ghost
Sitting on a post
Eating jam and hot-buttered toast.

12 The Little Red Hen

Once upon a time there was a little red hen, who lived on a farm with her chicks. Little Red Hen was always busy. She worked hard from morning 'til night.

A cat and a dog lived on the farm too. The cat snoozed all day in the barn, and never caught any mice. The dog dozed in the yard and couldn't be bothered to bark. They were such a lazy pair!

One day Little Red Hen went to the barn to get a bag of corn. "Who will help me carry this corn to the mill?" asked Little Red Hen.

"Not me," said the cat.

"Not me," said the dog.

"Very well," said Little Red Hen, "I'll do it myself, and my chicks will help."

So they did. Little Red Hen and her chicks took the corn to the mill. The miller ground the grain into flour. Then Little Red Hen carried it all the way home.

"Who will help me bake a crusty loaf of bread?" asked Little Red Hen.

"Not me," said the cat.

"Not me," said the dog.

"Very well," said Little Red Hen, "I'll bake it myself, and my chicks will help."

So they did. Little Red Hen got a bowl and mixed the flour with some water. Then she kneaded the dough, patted it into shape and put it in the oven.

Soon there was a delicious smell of bread baking. It wafted over the farmyard to where the cat and dog were sleeping.

Sniff, sniff . . . aaarh! The cat got up and stretched.
The dog yawned and scratched his ear. And they both went to see Little Red Hen.

"Who will help me eat this crusty loaf?" asked Little Red Hen.

"I will!" said the cat.

"Me too!" said the dog.

"Oh no you won't!" said Little Red Hen. "I took the corn to the mill, and mixed the dough and baked the bread. I did all the work, and my chicks helped. So we will eat it up."

And they did. The lazy cat and the lazy dog didn't get a crust or a crumb. Not one crumb! Which probably served them right.

Family Photographs

Grandpa has some photographs
(He keeps them in a book)
And whenever we go visiting,
We open it and look
At all the aunts and uncles
And the cousins that we know,
Or photographs of Grandpa
That were taken long ago.

There's a special one of Granny
In a white and frilly dress,
With Grandpa in a funny suit
And all the wedding guests.

There's a silly one that Grandpa took
When Mum was only three . . .
It's strange to think that Mum and Dad
Were little once, like me.

But here's the one I like the best,
We turn the page and look
At my Birthday Party photograph -
The best one in the book!

14 The Early Bird

The early bird may catch a worm
Or so I've often heard,
But in a topsy-turvy world
The worm would catch the bird!

15 Hullabaloo!

Hullabaloo!
I've lost my shoe
Oh where, oh where can it be?
I've looked on the floor,
By my bed and the door,
And under the big settee.

Hullabaloo!
I've *found* my shoe,
Hiding on the stair.
But what bothers me,
I really can't see,
Who could have put it there!

16 Annie Little and the Wolf

One day a shepherdess called Annie Little was sitting on a hill looking after her sheep. The sheep were grazing happily and soon Annie Little grew bored.

She looked down the hill to the village and saw all the people busy at work. Then, I'm sorry to say, Annie Little played a trick on them. She stood up and shouted, "Wolf! Wolf! There's a wolf after my sheep."

Everyone in the village stopped what they were doing and ran to help. But when they got to the top of the hill, Annie Little laughed and said, "It was just a joke. There isn't a wolf. I tricked you."

Nobody thought it was funny, and they went off grumbling and complaining about wasting so much time.

A whole week went by. Annie Little sat with her sheep day after day, and nothing exciting happened. She was fed up and thought she would play a trick on the villagers again. So she shouted at the top of her voice, "Wolf! Wolf! There's a wolf after my sheep."

She sounded so frantic this time that all the villagers came running at once. Annie Little laughed at them all. "I was only joking!" she said.

It will not surprise you to know that everyone was hopping mad. They stomped back down the hill and were very angry indeed.

Then one day something awful happened. Annie Little was up on the hill when, she DID see a wolf. The hungry wolf came creeping out of the wood. *Sniff. Sniff. Sniff.*

"WOLF! WOLF!" shouted Annie Little. "Help, please help! A wolf really IS after my sheep."

Well, of course, the villagers had heard this before. So they just laughed and said, "You're not tricking us this time." They went on with what they were doing and took no notice of her. People won't trust someone who tells lies, even when they tell the truth.

That wolf chased Annie Little's sheep all over the place. And, as far as I know, she's still looking for them.

One, Two, Off to the Zoo

One, two
We're off to the zoo
Mummy is driving the car.
Daddy is trying to read the map
He says it can't be far.

Three, four
Open the door
We're here and at the gate.
When are the lions going to be fed?
I hope we're not too late.

Five, six
Dolphins do tricks
We all get soaking wet.
We look at the elephants, camels and bears
And a hippo I'd love for a pet.

Seven, eight
The monkeys are great
Swinging from tree to tree.
Then down some steps to the penguins' pool
To watch them having tea.

Nine, ten
Home again
As sleepy as can be.
There's so much to do
When we go to the zoo
I'm glad you came with me!

18 The Silly Billies

"I want you to go to the shops for me," said Mrs Goat to her billy kids one morning. Mrs Goat wrote down the things she wanted them to buy.

She put some money in a purse and gave them each a basket.

"Hurry there and back," said Mrs Goat.

"We will," said the billy kids. And they skipped off down the hill.

First they bought a bag of sugar. Then they went to the greengrocer.

"Six melons, please," said the first billy kid.

"And one lemon," said the other. The shopkeeper looked a little surprised, but she gave them what they asked for.

1 bag of
sugar
1 melon
6 lemons

The billy kids struggled up the hill. Their baskets were very heavy. When they got home, Mrs Goat said, "Now I can make some lemonade with the sugar and lemons. And afterwards, we'll have a slice of melon."

But, oh dear! When Mrs Goat looked in the baskets she said, "You silly billies. I wanted six LEMONS and one MELON." The billy kids looked at the shopping list again.

"We got the words muddled up," said the billy kids. "*That's* why our baskets were heavy." And they all laughed.

"Well, we can't have any lemonade," said Mrs Goat, "but we'll be eating melon all week!"

19 The Little Monsters

The little monsters Meeny, Miny and Mo all live on Planet Pongo. Everything is the wrong way round on Pongo. It's a very muddly place to live.

One summer it was snowing hard. Snow on Pongo isn't cold and white - it's warm and pink, like candyfloss. Meeny, Miny and Mo were at the beach making snowcastles.

They were so busy digging that they didn't see the tide going out. And when the tide goes OUT on Pongo, the sea comes IN.

"Help!" cried Meeny, Miny and Mo.

The little monsters couldn't swim, so they climbed on top of their snowcastles and waited to be rescued.

They hadn't been there long when a big wave swished round them, and a rock appeared. Then another and another, all in a row.

"Stepping stones," said Meeny. The little monsters were about to tread on them when Miny said,

"Look! Those stones are moving."

"And they're covered in SCALES!" said Mo.

Just then a friendly sea dragon popped its head out of the water. "Hop on my back," said the dragon. "I'll take you back to the shore."

So Meeny, Miny and Mo got home safely after all.

20 The Magic Porridge Pot

Many years ago a little girl called Flora Isadora lived in a town with her mother. They were poor and Flora Isadora was always hungry. One day there was nothing to eat except a dry crust of bread.

"Here, take this crust and make it last," said Flora Isadora's mother.

Flora Isadora took the crust and went to play. While she was playing, an old woman came along.

"I haven't eaten for days," said the old woman. "Can you give me some food?"

Well, Flora Isadora felt sorry for the old woman, so she gave her the crust of bread. In return the old woman gave Flora a cooking pot.

"Take this little pot," she said. "It's magic. It won't work for me, but it will for you. Whenever you're hungry, just say, 'Cook, little pot, cook!' and it will fill up with porridge. And when you have eaten enough just say, 'Stop, little pot, stop!' and it will stop."

Flora Isadora thanked the old woman and ran to her mother. She plonked the pot on the table and said the magic words, "Cook, little pot, cook!" And it did. It bubbled to the brim with creamy hot porridge.

"Delicious!" said Flora Isadora's mother, as she tasted a spoonful.

When they had both had second helpings, Flora Isadora said the magic words, "Stop, little pot, stop!" And it obeyed her at once.

There came a morning when Flora Isadora was with her friends in the park. By lunch time, Flora Isadora's mother was feeling peckish. So, she put the magic pot on the table and said,

"Little pot, cook!" Nothing happened. "I must have got that wrong," said Flora Isadora's mother. So she tried again. "Cook, little pot, cook!" she said.

This time the little pot filled with porridge, and Flora Isadora's mother ate all she could. But the pot went on filling . . .

"Stop! Stop, little pot!" said Flora Isadora's mother. But the magic pot did no such thing. Porridge bubbled right over the table and on to the floor. "Please stop, little pot," said Flora Isadora's mother.

Soon there was a stream of hot porridge pouring out of the door and into the street. It splashed past all the houses and down to the park, where Flora Isadora was playing.

As soon as she saw what was happening she shouted in her loudest voice, "STOP, LITTLE POT, STOP!" The little pot heard her all the way back to the house, and stopped. Then everyone in the street came out and filled their bowls with porridge, and ate 'til they were full.

(21) The Battle of the Buns

Sam and Wallace had been out fishing in *The Topsy Turvy*. Sam had caught a lot of fish, and they were chugging home for tea. The sea was calm and everything was peaceful until, *BANG!*

There was a loud explosion followed by three *boom-boom-booms*. It was the Saucy Pirates aboard *The Bag o' Bones*. They were taking pot-shots at the coastguard's hut.

"Bullseye!" roared Captain Scuttlebutt, as a cannonball went straight through a window.

"Yo-ho-ho!" sang Snitch and Snatch.

Sam looked and saw that the pirates weren't firing cannonballs. They were using currant buns. Maggot, the cook, had baked the buns that morning, but they were rock hard. Captain Scuttlebutt had broken his best gold tooth trying to eat one, and now the Saucy Pirates were using them for target practice. Sam turned *The Topsy-Turvy* round and headed towards the pirates.

CRASH! A currant bun landed on the deck. Wallace took cover under some fish.

"Stop it at once!" yelled Sam.

But the pirates didn't stop. Maggot staggered up on deck with another tray of beastly buns. Snitch loaded them into the barrel and Snatch fired the cannon. Wallace blocked his ears with two kippers. *BANG-BOOM-BOOM!*

Then Sam had an idea. As three more buns came whizzing towards him he grabbed a caught the buns before they landed. The Saucy Pirates were furious.

"Give us back our buns," cried Captain Scuttlebutt. "Certainly not," said Sam.

"Well, me hearties," said Captain Scuttlebutt, "give us some fish and we'll be off."

"Only if you promise to stop firing those buns," said Sam. "AND say sorry to the coastguard for breaking his window."

"Done!" roared Captain Scuttlebutt.

Just then, Wallace noticed the coastguard flashing a signal.

"What does it say?" asked Wallace.

"It says, EVERYONE COME TO TEA," said Sam.

"Full steam ahead!" said Wallace.

So they all went to see the coastguard, and had fish and chips for tea.

22 Three Little Kittens

Three little kittens
Put on their mittens
And boots with fur inside.
They sat on a sleigh
And glided away
Down a slippery slide.

Three little kittens
They lost their mittens
And tumbled off the sleigh.
"Now come back inside,"
Their poor mother cried.
"No more sledging today!"

23 Winter Trees

In summer when it's very hot
Trees are dressed in leaves.
In winter when it snows a lot . . .
They're BARE.
Freezy, breezy, trees.

 Birthday Baking

It's Little Bear's birthday today and Mrs Bear is baking a cake. She mixes eggs, flour, sugar and lots of butter in a bowl. *Wizz-whirr-wizz.*

Little Bear watches the beaters go round and round.

When the mixture is just right, Mrs Bear pours it into a tin. *Slup, slup, slup.*

"You can scrape the bowl if you like," she says. Little Bear licks a sticky paw.

"Ummm, yum!" he says.

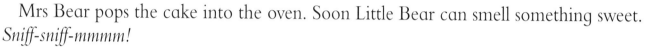 Mrs Bear pops the cake into the oven. Soon Little Bear can smell something sweet. *Sniff-sniff-mmmm!*

"Your cake must be cooked," says Mrs Bear. She puts on her mitts and takes it out of the oven. "Careful!" warns Mrs Bear. "It's hot."

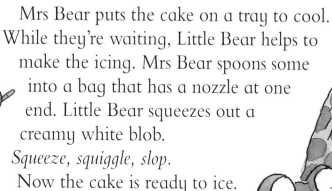 Mrs Bear puts the cake on a tray to cool. While they're waiting, Little Bear helps to make the icing. Mrs Bear spoons some into a bag that has a nozzle at one end. Little Bear squeezes out a creamy white blob. *Squeeze, squiggle, slop.*

Now the cake is ready to ice.

Mrs Bear covers it all over, and writes Happy Birthday Little Bear on the top.

When Little Bear's friends came to his party that day, Little Bear blew all his candles out in one go. *Huff, puff, pouff.*

And they each ate a big slice of delicious birthday cake.

📝 25 Sophie's Bed

One frosty night Sophie tucked her dolls and teddies into bed, and wriggled in beside them.

"Night, night, sleep tight. Don't let Jack Frost bite," said her mum.

"Who is Jack Frost?" asked Sophie sleepily.

"He paints frosty pictures on the window, and nips your nose with his fingers," said Sophie's mum.

Sophie lay in bed counting stars. The clear night sky was full of twinkling lights . . . and a voice whispered from her pillow,

Left, right, hold on tight. We're off to the Land of Dreams tonight.

"Who said that?" asked Sophie.

"Me," said the bed. "Here we go."

Sophie's bed got up on its bendy legs and flew out of the bedroom. They went over the rooftops, round the moon and landed on a star. It was the coldest place Sophie had ever been to.

By this time Sophie's bed had turned itself into a sleigh. They were gliding faster and faster towards a magnificent palace of ice. "That's Jack Frost's palace," explained the bed.

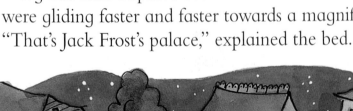

Before Sophie could say a word the icy walls CRACKED, and she found they were inside a freezing hall of icicles.

"Welcome," said a man, whose breath was as chilly as the North Wind. "You're just in time to help."

Jack Frost took them into a storeroom filled with tins of silver paint. Each glistening tin was labelled, FROSTY WHITE.

"Help me load up," said Jack Frost. "And don't forget the paintbrushes. I have to paint lots of windows before the sun comes up tomorrow."

But when Sophie's bed was piled high with paint, the bed whispered,

Left, right, hold on tight. Home again before morning light. ☆

And in two blinks they landed with a bump in her bedroom.

In the morning Sophie woke with a start. "I see Jack Frost has been here," said Mum. Sophie looked at the silvery patterns on the window. Then she saw something her mum hadn't noticed. There was a tiny silver paintbrush on the floor.

"Yes," said Sophie. "He has."

26 Katie's New School

Pa Purrkins was taking Katie kitten to school. It was her first day and Katie wondered what school would be like. She felt worried and excited at the same time.

"I don't feel well," said Katie.

"I expect it's just butterflies in your tummy," said Pa.

Mrs Tabby, the teacher, was waiting for Katie at the school door. She looked very friendly.

"Have a good time," said Pa, as he kissed Katie goodbye.

"I want to go home!" wailed Katie.

"Come along in," said Mrs Tabby. And she held Katie's paw.

When they got inside everyone was hanging up their coats. "This is your peg," said Mrs Tabby. It had Katie's name in big letters over the top, and a picture of an elephant underneath. Katie hung her coat on *her* peg. She liked elephants. She liked Mrs Tabby.

In the classroom Katie sat next to a kitten called Tim. They rolled modelling clay, painted pictures and built a house of bricks.

Then they drank milk, played dressing-up together, and listened to a story.

Pa Purrkins collected Katie at going home time. "How was school?" he asked.

"I've got a new friend called Tim," said Katie.

"That's nice," said Pa.

"Look. I painted a picture," said Katie.

"It's a very good elephant," said Pa. "Did you like school?"

"Yes," said Katie. "I can't wait until TOMORROW."

A Crumb

There's a crumb on my plate . . .

The plate is on a table

The table is in a room

The room is in a house

The house is in a street

The street is in a town

The town is in a country

The country is in the world.

And if the world were a plate . . .
that tiny crumb would be me.

I've Heard

Lions *roar,*

bears *growl,*

horses *neigh,*

cows *moo,*

hens *cluck,*

ducks *quack,*

chicks *cheep,*

mice *squeak* . . .

But I've never heard ants say
ANYTHING AT ALL.

29 Waiting

Police Constable Fox is holding up the traffic in the High Street today.
Honk honk. Beep beep. Parp parp!
"What's going on?" say all the drivers honking their horns and getting cross.
"Please be patient," says Constable Fox.
So, the bus on its way to school; a tanker taking petrol to the garage;
a taxi in a hurry to get to the airport; a tractor with a cart load of cabbages; a
truck full of stones to mend the road; a breakdown lorry towing a van and a
car full of noisy little monkeys . . .

all have to wait until Mrs Goosey Gander and her goslings have safely crossed the road!

30 Puddles

Town puddles
Street puddles
Soak through your feet puddles.
Cars *whoosh* through them
While we're waiting for the bus.

Farm puddles
Brown puddles
Gooey, squelchy warm puddles.
Ducks paddle in them
On flat webbed feet.

Rain puddles
Round puddles
Walking up and down puddles.
I *splash* through them
In my new rubber boots.

31 Shoe Shopping

Shopping for shoes
Which shall I choose?
The left shoe's all right,
But the right one's too tight.

This pair's a good fit
They don't pinch a bit
I wriggle my toes
And tie up the bows.

Then,

Walk round the shop
Once more and stop.
These red shoes look neat.
Just right for my feet.

Mum waits to pay
We take them away.
New shoes in a box
With a new pair of socks.

 A Colourful World

Sea swirling,
waves curling
blue.

Desert shifting,
sand drifting
yellow.

Seeds sowing,
grass mowing
green.

Fire burning,
flames turning
orange.

Wind blowing,
clouds growing
black.

Cold morning,
snow storming
white.

Sun setting,
sky getting
red.

Alfie

Alfie keeps taking my teddy
And biting his arm and his ear.
He's gone out of the door
With my sock in his jaw.
"Alfie, please bring it back here!"

Alfie loves chewing my shoes up.
He chewed my best slippers last week.
He sits on the stair
With ONE from each pair.
Alfie takes all the left feet.

Alfie is only a puppy
As naughty as puppies can be.
One day he'll grow up,
My lovable pup.
Alfie belongs to ME.

3 Greedy Mabel

Greedy Mabel
at the table
ate as much as
she was able.

Pies and pastries
cold or hot.
Greedy Mabel
scoffed the lot.

Chilli chicken,
fish in batter . . .
Wider Mabel grew
and fatter.

'Til at last
her mother said,
"Mabel it is
time for bed."

But when upon
the bed she sat.
Greedy Mabel's
bed fell flat.

It really couldn't
stand the weight,
from all that
Greedy Mabel ate.

Said Greedy Mabel
on her heels,
"I'll eat a little
LESS at meals!"

31

The Old Witch

There was an old witch
Lived under a hill,
And if she's not gone
She lives there still.

She flys at night
By the light of the moon,
And if she's not gone
She'll be home soon . . .

So you'd better RUN.

The Giant

Fee, fi, fo, fum,
A giant was here in town.
His great big feet
Clumped down our street,
Knocking the houses down.

Fee, fi, fo, fum,
The giant had come for ME.
His mouth opened wide,
He popped me inside
And crunched my bones for tea.

Fee, fi, fo, fum,
You must have heard me scream.
"You're safe in bed,"
My father said.
"That giant was in your DREAM."

6 The Wrong Throat Sweets

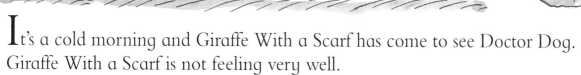

It's a cold morning and Giraffe With a Scarf has come to see Doctor Dog. Giraffe With a Scarf is not feeling very well.

"I've got a sore throat," he says.

Doctor Dog wants to look at his patient's throat properly, but he can't reach. Giraffe With a Scarf has a very long neck.

"Wait there," says Nurse Kitty. And she fetches a ladder.

Doctor Dog climbs to the top of the ladder. He looks all the way down the throat with his special torch.

"You need some Extra Strong throat sweets," Doctor Dog tells his patient.

Nurse Kitty is standing at the bottom of the ladder.

"I'll get some straightaway," she says.

Nurse Kitty goes to the place where all the medicines are kept.

She is there for quite a time. Doctor Dog and Giraffe With a Scarf come to see what Nurse Kitty is doing.

"I'm sticking these throat sweets together," explains Nurse Kitty. "You asked for Extra Long ones."

Doctor Dog and Giraffe With a Scarf laugh their heads off.

"I said, Extra STRONG throat sweets," says Doctor Dog.

"Oh dear!" says Nurse Kitty. "I must have misheard you."

"Well," says Giraffe With a Scarf, "it's a good job you did. All that laughing has made me feel much better. I won't need those Extra *Long* sweets after all!"

7 Princess Bossy Boots

Priscilla was bossy. She bossed everybody.

"Put your crown on straight!" she said to the king. "I want a new dress NOW," she told the queen. "Come here . . . do this . . . do that," she ordered the palace servants. No wonder everyone secretly called her Princess Bossy Boots.

On her sixth birthday, the princess had a party. Now a wizard had heard all about Princess Bossy Boots, so he decided to give her a special present - just right for someone with bossy ways.

When he arrived, the princess and her friends were playing in the ballroom. The princess was having a lovely time ordering her guests about.

"Oh good, another present," she said, rudely snatching the box from the wizard.

Princess Bossy Boots tore off the paper and took out the prettiest pair of boots she had ever seen.

She put them on straightaway. No sooner had she tied the laces than the boots grinned at each other.

"Best foot forward," said the right boot.

"Quick march!" said the left boot. "Left, right. Left, right."

"Hey!" said Princess Bossy Boots, "I give the orders round here."

The boots took no notice.

"Ready for a run?" asked the right boot.

"No!" said the princess.

"Yes," said the left boot.

Off they ran, across a muddy field and up

a hill. Princess Bossy Boots was soon out of breath, but the boots ran on and on.

At last they marched the tired and bedraggled princess back to the palace. The wizard was waiting for her.

"TAKE THESE STUPID BOOTS AWAY!" she cried.

"Only if you say *please*," said the wizard.

Princess Bossy Boots had never said that little word before. She looked down at the boots. They were itching to be off again . . .

"PLEASE!" she shouted. And, as if by magic, the boots vanished.

Ever since that day, Princess Priscilla always says, 'please' and 'thank you', and has never been bossy again!

8 My New Brother

I've got a new baby brother;
Mark's AWFUL and makes such a noise.
Dad says he's great.
Mum thinks he's sweet.
I really don't like little boys.

Mark makes a real mess at mealtimes,
He tips all his food on his head.
Gran thinks he's fine,
Gramps says he's grand.
I giggle a *bit* when he's fed.

Last Monday Mark grew a new tooth.
On Friday he started to crawl.
My friends think he's fun,
My sister agrees.
I *suppose* he's quite nice, after all.

My brother's just had his First Birthday.
I gave him a card and a toy.
There'll be lots he can do,
When I'm five and he's two.
I'm *glad* my brother's a boy.

9 Twice As Much

Alex is my best friend
Sometimes we don't agree.
If I've got one thing
He's got more.
Twice as much as me.

I said, "I've got two rabbits,
We keep them in a hutch."
He has four
You see, that's more.
Exactly twice as much.

We fell over running.
I tripped and grazed my leg.
My knee hurt
His hurt *most*.
"Twice as much," he said.

But last week I got sick.
I had ONE HUNDRED spots.
We counted up
And he had NONE.
I'd twice as much . . . BY LOTS!

10 Hurry Up!

"Lucy, we're waiting to go to the park," said Mrs MacGee, who was helping with the children one afternoon.

"I'm coming," said Lucy.

"What *are* you doing?" said Mrs MacGee.

"I've lost my shoes."

"Well hurry up and find them," said Mrs MacGee.

"I can't."

"Look under the bed," said Mrs MacGee.

"I have."

"I'm counting to five," said Mrs MacGee. "If you don't find your shoes and put them on by then, we'll go to the swings without you. One."

"Found them."

"Two," said Mrs MacGee.

"I can't get the laces undone."

"You should have untied them *before* you took them off last time," said Mrs MacGee. "Three."

"Stop counting. It's not fair. I've undone them now."

"Four," said Mrs MacGee..

"I've got to do the bows."

"Four-and-a-half," said Mrs MacGee.

"I've done one. I'm *nearly* ready."

"F-f-f . . ." said Mrs MacGee.

"Wait!"

"FIVE," said Mrs MacGee.

"Done it!" said Lucy proudly.

And they all went off to the park.

11 The Farmer, the Wife and the Old Grey Mare

Once long ago a farmer and his wife were taking their old grey mare to market. The farmer walked in front, his wife behind and the old grey mare in the middle. The farmer went *trudge-trudge,* the wife went *hobble-hobble,* and the mare went *clippy clip-clop!*

On the road they met a little girl. She was looking for her dog and wasn't in a very friendly mood. "How stupid!" she said when she saw the farmer and his wife. "Fancy having a horse and not riding it."

The farmer thought she was right. So he rode the mare and his wife walked behind. The wife went *hobble-hobble,* and the mare went *clippy clip-clop!*

Soon they reached town and passed two boys called Tom Tittle and Tim Tattle. They were having an argument. But when they saw the farmer riding, and his wife hobbling behind, Tom and Tim stopped arguing and said, "What a selfish man." They both agreed on that.

So the farmer told his wife to climb up too. And the mare went *clippy clip-clop!*

Just then a thief came running down the street with a pig. He stopped when he saw the farmer and his wife on the old grey mare. "Poor horse!" cried the thief. "She'll never get to market with you two lumps for a load."

So the farmer and his wife got off. They tied the mare's legs together with rope and slung her on a pole. The farmer went *trudge-trudge* and the wife went *hobble-hobble* and they CARRIED that old grey mare to market.

When they got there, all the people laughed and laughed to see such a silly sight. So the farmer and his wife dropped the old grey mare and RAN. Which only goes to show that you can't please everybody.

And as for the old grey mare . . . a kind lady took her home and looked after her very well. *CLIPPY CLIP-CLOP!*

12 What a Noise!

There was once a farmer called Joe Barley who lived with his wife, Betty, in a little cottage. They had four children and Betty Barley was always complaining about the cottage being too small.

The children were a quarrelsome lot too, so what with the nagging and the squabbling Joe got no peace at all.

Now there was an old Scarecrow on the farm. The Scarecrow wasn't much good at frightening the birds, but he was very wise. Joe often went to see him, to tell him his troubles.

One day the Scarecrow said, "I've been thinking about your problem. Do you have any chickens?"

"Of course," said Joe. "Six speckled hens and a cockerel."

"Good," said the Scarecrow. "Take them into your cottage and see what happens."

Joe thought this was an odd idea, but he was willing to try anything for a quiet life. So he did as the Scarecrow had said. But all day long the cock crowed; the hens cackled; the children argued and Betty Barley moaned more than ever. What a noise!

"It's not working," said Joe when he saw the Scarecrow again.

"How about goats?" asked the Scarecrow. "Do you have any?"

"I've got a billy goat and a nanny goat," said Joe.

"Put them in your cottage and see what happens," said the Scarecrow.

Well the goats bleated and ate everything in sight; the cock crowed; the hens cackled; the children were miserable and Betty Barley grumbled bitterly.

"I've got enough to put up with without you bringing home more trouble," she said. "You empty-headed fool! You've got about as much sense as that Scarecrow you keep talking to."

"Things are much worse," Joe told the Scarecrow later. "It's so noisy and smelly and full of messy animals. This can't be right."

"There's just one more thing," said the Scarecrow. "Do you have a cow?"

"What!" said Joe. "I have one brown-eyed cow who gives us milk each morning but . . ."

"Trust me," said the Scarecrow. "Take the brown-eyed cow into your cottage and see what happens."

So Joe took the brown-eyed cow into the cottage. It was terrible. The cow mooed and trod on everyone's toes; the goats bleated and ate everything in sight; the cock crowed; the hens cackled; the children were crying and Betty Barley shouted,

"ENOUGH. Take all these animals out of the cottage at once."

And this is what happened; Joe took the brown-eyed cow who gave milk each morning, the billy goat and the nanny goat, the six speckled hens and the cockerel all back to the farmyard. Betty Barley and the children cleared up the mess and, by bedtime that night, they said,

"LISTEN. It's so peaceful. We have plenty of room now all those noisy animals have gone."

Joe crept out of the cottage next day and went to see the Scarecrow.

"It worked!" said Joe. "It's so quiet at home, you can hear a pin drop."

"I'm very glad to hear it," said the Scarecrow with a wink.

My Picture

I've drawn the house I live in
It has a chimney pot,
A roof, four windows and a door -
That's what my house has got.

I've drawn a garden round it -
Six flowers and a tree.
The path goes up the middle
As straight as it can be.

I've coloured-in my drawing
The sky is deepest blue.
And now my picture's ready
To show to all of you.

I hope you like it.

39

14 Mrs Bear's Valentine

"It's Valentine's Day today," says Mrs Bear one morning.

"I know," says Little Bear. "The postman has brought you a card. It's got a heart on the envelope."

Mrs Bear opens it at once and reads it out loud;

Roses are red,
Violets are blue,
Honey is sweet
And so are you!

"Now, I wonder who that's from?" says Mrs Bear with a smile. "There's a smudgy paw mark at the bottom."

Just then Little Bear sees something outside the window. "Look," he says, "there's a jar of honey walking up the garden path." Mrs Bear goes to the window. Somebody with furry paws is carrying the biggest jar of honey she has ever seen. It has,

To My Valentine

in large letters on the label.

Little Bear opens the door and the jar of honey walks in.

"Daddy!" says Little Bear. "It's you."

"My Valentine," says Mrs Bear. And she gives Mr Bear a big hug.

Then Mr Bear, Mrs Bear and Little Bear all sit down and have hot waffles and honey for a special breakfast on Valentine's Day.

15 Four Black Crows

Four black crows
Sitting in a tree.
One flapped off -
Then there were three.

One croaked, Caw!
And away he flew.
Count on your fingers -
That left two.

Two black crows
Up on a bough.
One fell over -
How many now?

One black crow
All on his own.
Perched on a scarecrow -
Then there were none.

16 Off to Sea

We're going to sea in my bed boat
I've rigged up a sort of a sail.
I expect we'll meet lots of pirates
And I'm hoping to see a whale.

I've packed my sweets and some biscuits
The crew are all lined up on deck.
I've got my swim things and flippers,
We're sure to find a shipwreck.

Now my bed boat is ready,
"Up anchor! We're off to sea."

Then,

Dad calls me into the kitchen.
We'll have to explore AFTER tea.

⟦17⟧ The Good Idea

Three little mice called Hop, Skip and Jumpy were having a meeting one night. They were trying to think what to do about Big Ginger, the cat.

"There is delicious cheese in the kitchen," said Hop. "But we dare not go in."

"Big Ginger is always on the prowl," said Skip.

"If only we knew when she was about," said Jumpy. "She treads so softly on her paws, we never hear her coming."

And that gave Hop an idea.

"We could put a bell on Big Ginger's collar," he said. "It would jingle whenever she walked, and we would hear her."

"Then we could have cheese every night," said Skip.

"And run before she catches us!" squeaked Jumpy excitedly.

They all agreed it was a very good idea.

"There's just one thing . . ." said Hop slowly. "Who will put the bell on Big Ginger's collar ?"

There was silence.

"Well, I thought of the plan," said Hop. "So I have done my bit."

"My eyesight is poor," said Skip. "I wouldn't be able to fix the bell on properly."

"And I'm too small," said Jumpy. "I couldn't lift the bell to put it on her collar."

So, since not one of those three mice were willing to put the bell on Big Ginger's collar, they all scampered back to their holes.

The Moon in the River

Early one evening the billy kids were walking home across the fields. The winter days were short and it had grown dark.

They were crossing the bridge over the river, when one billy kid said,

"Look. The moon has fallen in the water." They leaned over and stared at the bright silvery moon, bobbing in the river below.

While they were looking at it, Rabbit came hopping over the bridge.

"The moon has fallen in the water," said the billy kids.

"Goodness me," said Rabbit. And he hopped away smiling.

Soon afterwards Wriggly Snake and Mole crossed over the bridge. The billy kids told them about the moon too.

"Isss that s-s-so!" said Wriggly Snake, squiggling with giggles. Then she and Mole went off laughing.

At that moment Owl flew down.

"Look," said the billy kids. "The moon IS in the water. No one will believe us."

Owl smiled. "You silly billies," he said. "Look up in the sky. *There's* the moon! The one in the river is just a REFLECTION."

Then the billy kids ran all the way home - by the light of the moon.

19 The Snowman

Granny Simpkin lived all by herself in a busy town. Every day people hurried by her house on their way to work. But no one came to see her, and Granny Simpkin was lonely.

One winter's day it snowed. Snowflakes fell thick and fast and covered everything in a crisp white blanket. When it stopped, Granny Simpkin put on her boots and went into the garden.

Then, just for fun, she made a snowman and called him Mr Snow.

"I've no one else to talk to," said Granny Simpkin as she put a hat on his head and wrapped a long woolly scarf round his neck. She found a walking stick and gave him that too.

"Thank you," said Mr Snow.

For the next few days, while it was still cold, Granny Simpkin and Mr Snow chatted away together. They got on very well.

One afternoon Granny Simpkin went out to the shops. While she was away, an old man came down the street. He was shabbily dressed in a tatty torn coat, and he felt cold. When the old man got to Granny Simpkin's house and saw the snowman he said,

"That's a fine hat you're wearing."

Mr Snow felt sorry for him.

"You may have it," said Mr Snow. "Cold weather doesn't bother me at all."

So the old man thanked the snowman and put on the hat.

"That scarf looks warm," said the old man.

"Please take it," said Mr Snow. "To tell you the truth, it was making me too hot."

The old man put on the scarf. Then he slipped on the icy path.

"You'd better have my stick as well," said Mr Snow. "I'm not going anywhere. You need it more than I do."

By now the old man was feeling much better. He thanked the snowman again, and said he would come the next day. The old man was lonely too.

That night the weather changed. In the morning the sun shone brightly on

Mr Snow and, by lunch time he had melted. Granny Simpkin was sad. She was puzzled, too. Mr Snow's hat, scarf and walking stick were nowhere to be seen.

Just then the old man stopped outside Granny Simpkin's house.

"Now there's a thing," said Granny Simpkin. "Mr Snow had a hat and a scarf and a walking stick, just like yours."

So the old man whose name was George, told her what had happened.

"Well," said Granny Simpkin "you're very welcome to those things. Mr Snow won't be needing them any more."

"*I* could come and see you every day," said George. "I live at the other end of the street."

"That *would* be nice," said Granny Simpkin. "Come to tea tomorrow. I'll bake a cake."

After that George and Granny Simpkin became very good friends, and were never lonely again.

20 Ladywig and Earbird

A ladywig and earbird
Were crawling up the wall.
Said the earbird to the ladywig,
"I don't feel right at all."

Said the ladywig, "I feel odd too
Now this may seem absurd,
But at the top
Our names we'll swap,
EARWIG and LADYBIRD."

"You've changed my life!"
The earwig said,
"I feel a different bug."
Then the earwig gave the ladybird
A great big buggy hug.

21 Dinosaur Spellings

Dinosaurs have such strange names.
They're long and not easy to spell like,

STEGOSAURUS

TRICERATOPS

PTERODACTYL
and
TYRANNOSAURUS
as well.

But dinosaur names are *special*
So I'm trying my hardest to spell,

STEGOSAURUS

TRICERATOPS

PTERODACTYL
and
TYRANNOSAURUS
as well!

Noah's Bedsocks

It was a cold night and Noah was getting ready for bed. He put on his warmest nightgown and a pair of woolly bedsocks. He was climbing into bed, when he heard the sound of sobbing outside his window.

"*Tu-whit, tu-whoo, tu-BOO-hoo-hoo.*"

Noah got up to see who was crying. He opened the window and saw two little owls in a tree.

"We're very cold," sobbed the little owls.

Noah felt sorry for them and wondered how he could help. He looked down at his bedsocks and thought for a moment - and he had an idea.

Noah got a spare pair of bedsocks out of his drawer, and told the little owls to come inside. Then he popped one little owl into each sock and hung the socks on the end of his bed.

"We're lovely and warm," sang the little owls happily.

"Good," said Noah. "Now for some sleep."

"*Tu-whit, tu-whoo.*"

"Oh no!" said Noah. "I've just remembered something . . .owls STAY AWAKE all night."

"*Tu-whit, tu-whoo, tu-HOO-HOO-HOO!*"

47

23 Opposites

Fast as a spaceship,
　　　slow as a snail,
Big as a dinosaur,
　　　small as a nail.
Fierce as a tiger,
　　　gentle as a lamb,
Sour as a lemon,
　　　sweet as jam.
Dry as the desert,
　　　wet as the sea,
Square as a house,
　　　round as a pea.
Cool as a cave,
　　　warm as toast,
Noisy as a road drill,
　　　quiet as a ghost.
Strong as an ox,
　　　weak as a kitten,
Hard as a rock,
　　　soft as a mitten.
Dark as a tunnel,
　　　light as the moon,
Night time midnight,
　　　day time noon.
Tall as a giant,
　　　short as an elf,
Crooked as a mountain path,
　　　straight as a shelf . . .

The world is full of opposites,
　　　so think of some yourself!

24 Pig Wigs

Penelope Grigg is
a vain little pig.
Each day she is wearing
a different wig.

A pink wig on Monday.
On Tuesday, a green –
the silliest pig wig
you ever have seen.

On Wednesday she chooses
a wig with long curls.
On Thursday a straight one
that slips when she twirls.

On Friday Penelope
runs to keep fit,
in one tied with toggles
and bobbles and bits.

Her Saturday wig
was bought in a sale.
And on Sunday Miss Grigg
wears a piggy wig tail.

The Runaway Elephant

One day Stripy Tiger was asleep under the Tum Tum tree. The monkeys were playing in the branches above.

Suddenly one of the monkeys gave a shout. This was followed by the sound of something running through the wood. *Thump-thump, thump-thump.* It was Baby Elephant. The ground shook as he pounded along the path trumpeting noisily.

Stripy Tiger woke up just as Baby Elephant got to the Tum Tum tree. *Thump-thump, thump-thump,* thump!

"Owwwch!" yelled Stripy Tiger as a large foot trod on his tail. Baby Elephant thought Stripy Tiger would be cross, so he ran off.

Stripy Tiger was still examining his tail, when Police Constable Fox came by. He pinned a notice to the Tum Tum tree. It said;

LOST ONE BABY ELEPHANT

The monkeys and Stripy Tiger read the notice carefully.

"Has anyone seen Mrs Elephant's baby?" said Police Constable Fox.

"Seen and *felt* him," said Stripy Tiger. "He was a very heavy baby."
He explained what had happened, and Police Constable Fox said,
"I must look for him at once."

Stripy Tiger and the monkeys offered to help.

"You go one way, and I'll go the other," said Police Constable Fox, "and we'll meet at the Tum Tum tree." So that is what they did.

Meanwhile, in another part of the wood, Baby Elephant had been going round and round in circles. He was lost and frightened, and wished more than anything that he hadn't run away from his mother. He sat down and cried. Large tears rolled down his cheeks and dripped off the end of his trunk.

He was still there when the monkeys spotted him.

"There he is, behind that bush," they shouted. Stripy Tiger bounced up to the little elephant.

"Come along," he said. "You can hold on to my tail." Baby Elephant was pleased to see him.

"I'm sorry I trod on your tail," he said.

"That's all right," said Stripy Tiger. "It's better now." And he took the little elephant back to the Tum Tum tree.

Police Constable Fox and Mrs Elephant were waiting for them. Mrs Elephant thanked everyone for finding her baby. Then they both trotted off happily.

Thump-thump. THUMP, THUMP, THUMP!

49

26 Katie's Mouse

It was a dull grey day and Katie kitten had nothing to do.

"I'm bored," said Katie.

"Come and help me tidy my treasure chest," said Ma Purrkins.
She opened a box full of odds and ends.

"These will all come in useful one day," said Ma tipping everything on to
the table.

Among the pile were scraps of felt, buttons, pot-lids, cards and a ball of string.
The string had got in a tangle, so Ma unravelled the knots and Katie helped to wind it up.

"What I need is a string holder," said Ma. "I saw one that looked like a mouse in a jumble sale. I wish
I'd bought it."

"We could make one," said Katie.

"That's a good idea," said Ma.

Ma helped Katie sort through all the 'treasure' to find the things they
would need. Katie drew round a pot-lid and made two mouse bodies
from scraps of felt. Ma found a needle and thread and helped to sew
on ears, two button eyes and a nose. Then Katie stitched the two
body shapes together, neatly round the edge.

"My mouse needs a tail," said Katie.

"I'm coming to that," said Ma. She pushed the ball of string
through a slit at the back, and poked the end of it through a hole.
"Pull the string," said Ma.

Katie pulled the string out a little way.

"Now my mouse has got a tail," she said.

"And I've got a new string holder," said Ma Purrkins.
"Thank you very much."

27 Tucker and the Apple Tree

There was once a little pony called Tucker, who shared a field with Alice, the donkey. There was plenty of long green grass for them to eat, but Tucker was greedy. He was always looking for tasty tit-bits on the other side of the fence.

One morning Tucker saw an apple tree. He hadn't noticed it before.

"Those apples look juicy," he said to Alice.

"You'll never reach them," said Alice. "Your legs are too short and the branches are too high."

"Well, I'm going to try," said Tucker.

He leaned against the fence and stretched his neck. The apples bobbed about in the breeze, well out of reach.

Tucker tried again. This time he put his two front hooves on the fence. He stretched and wobbled, and tried his best to nibble the nearest branch. But he COULD NOT pull those apples down.

"Told you so," said Alice at last. Tucker pretended not to care.

"I've changed my mind about those apples," he said. "They look very sour and much too small to bother about."

Hm! thought Alice. You're only saying that because you *can't* have them. But instead she said, "Come on. I know where there's a big clump of thistles we can *both* have!"

And they galloped off together.

28 The New Witch

The day Hilda Brimstone moved into Moonshine Mansions, Alfred Jones just knew she was a witch. He actually saw a broomstick and a cat amongst her luggage.

Alfred told his friend Mr Hargreaves who lived on the ground floor.

"Good," said Mr Hargreaves. "We could do with some magic round here."

Next day Alfred went to see his new neighbour. He climbed to the top floor of Moonshine Mansions and knocked on the door. It opened all by itself.

"I'm Alfred Jones," said Alfred.

"I'm in the middle of a spell," said Hilda.

"Coo!" said Alfred. "Can I watch?"

"Of course," said Hilda. "Come in."

Hilda Brimstone was trying to magic some breakfast for her cat, Hubble. He had asked for sardines. Hilda clicked her fingers . . .*Snap!* and two medium-sized submarines appeared in his bowl.

"I must have got that wrong somehow," said Hilda.

"Typical," said Hubble. "I'll go and catch a mouse."

That evening Alfred told his mum about Hilda Brimstone. "She's a real witch," he said.

"You mustn't be rude about people," said Mrs Jones. So Alfred never mentioned her again.

Alfred went to visit Hilda nearly every day. He told her all about his friend, Mr Hargreaves.

"I feel really sorry for him," said Alfred.

"Why?" said Hilda.

"Mr Hargreaves loves gardening," said Alfred. "He used to have a big garden. Now he's stuck in a wheelchair and can't get out much."

"Hm, let me see . . ." said Hilda thumbing through her spell book. "I may be able to help."

So Alfred took Hilda to meet Mr Hargreaves. He was busy watering a window-box when they arrived.

Hilda looked at the window-box and clicked her fingers twice. *Snip! Snap!* There was a puff of smoke and . . . suddenly the room was full of gigantic leafy plants and exotic flowers.

"I think I may have overdone it," said Hilda struggling through some creepers.

"It's FANTASTIC!" said Mr Hargreaves. "You're the best witch in the world."

At bedtime, Alfred told his mum what had happened. "Mr Hargreaves has got a jungle in his sitting-room," he said.

"You and your stories," said Mrs Jones. "First we have a witch living on the top floor. And now there's a jungle at the bottom."

And she kissed Alfred goodnight.

# My Real Birthday

Birthdays come round once a year
That's not quite true of mine.
My birthday falls in Leap Year
On February twenty-nine.

Four years ago, when I was born
My life had just begun.
This is my FIRST real birthday
But I am *four* - not one.

I have a birthday every year
So I grow up on time.
But my *real* one's every four years,
On February twenty-nine.

1 All Patched Up

One morning the telephone rings in Doctor Dog's surgery. It's Mrs Pig and she sounds worried.

"Please come," says Mrs Pig. "Mr Pig has fallen off a ladder."

Doctor Dog rushes to his car. He must get to Mr Pig quickly.

"Oh dear!" says Nurse Kitty. "He's left all these bandages behind." Nurse Kitty puts the bandages and plenty of sticking plasters into a bag. Then she gets on her bicycle and pedals after him.

Meanwhile Doctor Dog has found Mr Pig sitting at the bottom of the ladder. He looks very sorry for himself. A hammer and lots of nails are scattered in the road.

"I was mending my roof," he explains. Doctor Dog examines Mr Pig carefully.

"No bones broken," says Doctor Dog. "Just a few bumps and bruises."

Then Nurse Kitty arrives and soon Mr Pig is bandaged up. But when Doctor Dog goes to drive his car away - he can't move at all. The nails in the road have punctured his tyres. They are as flat as pancakes.

Nurse Kitty has an idea. She takes some sticking plasters out of her bag and patches the holes. Then she gets her bicycle pump and fills the tyres full of air.

"Now we're all patched up!" laughs Doctor Dog, as he drives away.

3 Jack Sprat's Cat

Jack Sprat (I'm sure you know)
Could not eat any fat.
But here's a tale you may enjoy
About Jack's cunning cat.

While Jack ate all the lean meat
Joan Sprat enjoyed the fat;
And any scraps left over
Were given to the cat.

One day when they went out
The cat was left alone.
The meat was on the table
So she ate it on her own.

When Jack and Joan came back
They shook their fists and cried
The cat was fast asleep
With all the meat inside!

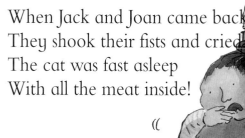

2 Elfish Nonsense

As I was sitting in my chair
I saw an elf who wasn't there.
He spoke, but didn't say a word
His silent voice was all I heard.
He didn't come again today.
I wish that elf would go away!

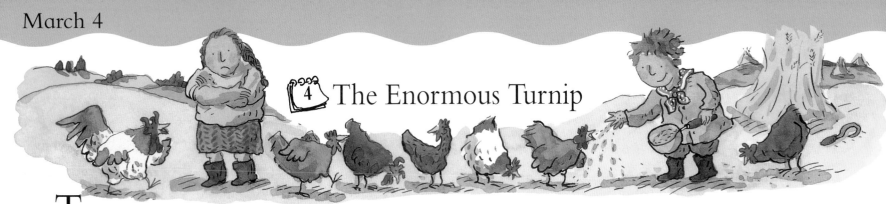

4 The Enormous Turnip

There was once a man called Tom Tickle. He grew the best corn for his hens and the cock-a-dooley bird, but he never grew anything for his wife.

Tom Tickle's wife complained, so Tom planted a turnip seed. Sure enough the seed began to grow. It grew . . . and it grew . . . and it grew . . . until one day it had grown into an enormous turnip.

Tom Tickle's wife was as pleased as anything.

"We shall have turnip for dinner tonight," she said.

Tom Tickle went to pull the turnip up. He grabbed the turnip by the top. He heaved, tugged and pulled, but the turnip wouldn't budge.

"Trust you to plant a thing like that," complained his wife.

"Well, come and help," said Tom Tickle. So, the wife held on to Tom Tickle and Tom Tickle grabbed the turnip. They heaved, tugged and pulled, but the turnip wouldn't budge.

Aunt Jelly came out of the house to see what they were doing.

"Please come and help," said Tom Tickle. So, Aunt Jelly caught hold of the wife, the wife held on to Tom Tickle and Tom Tickle grabbed the turnip.

They heaved, tugged and pulled, but the turnip wouldn't budge.

Now it happened that Rosie the Robber came by. She had been up to some no good robbing business, and was being chased by a skinny thin dog with a flea on its tail.

Rosie the Robber was tired of being chased. She tossed her sack of stolen goodies over the fence and came to help. The dog didn't want to miss the fun, so he came too.

The skinny thin dog with a flea on its tail hung on to Rosie the Robber, Rosie the Robber clung on to Aunt Jelly, Aunt Jelly caught hold of the wife, the wife held on to Tom Tickle and Tom Tickle grabbed the turnip.

They heaved, tugged and pulled, but still that turnip wouldn't budge.

Just then a teeny wee mouse came scampering along and he took hold of the skinny thin dog's tail and PULLED.

And UP came that enormous turnip at last!

That evening Tom Tickle, his wife, Aunt Jelly, Rosie the Robber, the skinny thin dog with a flea on its tail and the teeny wee mouse all ate that enormous turnip for dinner - and there was plenty for the hens and the cock-a-dooley bird too.

5 Listen!

Sirens *wail*
Cymbals *clash*
Doors *bang*
Waves *crash*.

Twigs *snap*
Plates *clatter*
Fires *crackle*
Children *chatter*.

Bees *hum*
Birds *sing*
Kettles *whistle*
Bells *ring*.

Cats *purr*
Locks *click*
Dreamers *sigh*
Clocks *tick . . . tick . . . tick . . .*

6 The Wind, the Sun and Nimble Simon

One day the Wind and the Sun were having an argument. The Wind was boasting about how strong he was. The Sun smiled and said,

"You can huff and puff as much as you like. I am stronger than you."

The Wind looked around and saw a boy walking to the fair. He was wearing a coat.

"Look," said the Wind. "Let's see which one of us can make that boy take off his coat, before he gets to the fair. We'll soon see who's more powerful."

The Wind took a deep breath, puffed out his cheeks and blew. The sudden gust swept the boy, who was called Nimble Simon, off his feet.

"Dear me," he said getting up and buttoning his coat.

Then the Wind turned his face to the North. He sucked in the icy cold air from the top of the world and blew even harder. This time a furious storm of hailstones beat down from the clouds.

"Oh help!" cried Nimble Simon.   He turned up his collar, pulled the coat more tightly round him and started running.

The Wind blew 'til there wasn't a breath of air left in him. But he COULD NOT make the boy take off his coat.

"My turn now," said the Sun.

He shone down out of a bright blue sky. Golden rays of sunshine fell on the boy's shoulders, and he felt warm. Nimble Simon undid one coat button . . .

The Sun beamed all over his face and shone brighter than ever. It grew hotter and hotter.

"Phew!" said Nimble Simon. And he undid two coat buttons . . .

The Sun blazed away. The fair was just around the corner, when Nimble Simon said, "I can't take another step in this coat. I'm much too hot!" So he undid three coat buttons and . . .

TOOK THE COAT RIGHT OFF.

"There!" said the Sun to the Wind. "I've won. My gentle ways were better than all your angry huffing and puffing."

The Wind scowled, but he had to admit the Sun was right.

Nimble Simon looked up at the Wind and the Sun and said, "You two! I wish you'd make your mind up about the weather today."

Then he ran to the fair, and spent all afternoon on the roundabouts.

Hair Care

Long hair
Short hair
Curly or not.
Plait in a pigtail
Bunch on top.

Silk strands
Rubber bands
Combs and clips.
Ruffles and ribbons with
Toggles on the tips.

Black hair
Red hair
Dark or fair.
Count to ONE HUNDRED
When you brush your hair.

Flower Pots

The bulbs we plant in autumn
Flower in the spring.
Like daffodils and hyacinths –
They grow like anything.

It doesn't seem to matter
If the weather's fine or not.
Just put them on a windowsill
To flower in a pot!

59

Twenty Knobbly Knees

Twenty knobbly knees
Nineteen fidgety fleas
Eighteen building bricks
Seventeen chirpy chicks
Sixteen squiggly snakes
Fifteen fancy cakes
Fourteen flying bats
Thirteen hanging hats
Twelve croaky frogs
Eleven slippery logs
Ten teddy bears
Nine old chairs
Eight twinkling stars
Seven racing cars
Six bright coats
Five sailing boats
Four favourite books
Three quarrelling cooks
Two ticking clocks
One odd sock

📅 10 One Drop

Mr Skinny Flint was the meanest man in the world. He lived in a tumbledown house because he was much too mean to mend it. His trousers were full of holes because he was too mean to buy a new pair. And, when Mr Skinny Flint went shopping, he bought one small potato and half a loaf of bread - to last all week.

It wasn't that Mr Skinny Flint was poor. Oh no! He had lots of money saved up in jam jars, which he kept under his bed. But of course, he was much too mean to spend it.

One day a woman knocked at Mr Skinny Flint's door. He opened the door a little way, and peered out.

"Please may I have some water?" asked the woman. "I have been walking all day and I'm very thirsty."

"No!" said Mr Skinny Flint. And he slammed the door shut. *Bang.*

The woman tried again. This time Mr Skinny Flint said grudgingly, "Oh, all right." He went to the kitchen and came back with a cup. It had one drop of water in it. One drop! You see how mean he was?

"That's not much of a drink," said the woman. And she went away.

Next day the weather turned cold. Mr Skinny Flint lit a small fire in his sitting-room. But he had been much too mean to have the chimney cleaned, and it caught fire. Mr Skinny Flint telephoned the Fire Brigade.

"Come quickly!" he shouted. "My chimney is on fire."

The Fire Brigade sent a fire engine at once.

"Only one fire engine?" said Mr Skinny Flint.

"Only one chimney pot," replied the fire officer, who looked strangely like the woman who had called on him the day before.

The fire officer ran up the garden path with a hosepipe. She turned on the water, and put ONE DROP of water on the fire.

"One drop!" shouted Mr Skinny Flint. "That's no good."

"Well, that's all you're getting," said the fire officer, "unless . . ."

"Unless what?" said Mr Skinny Flint crossly.

"Unless you promise not to be so mean in future."

Mr Skinny Flint looked up at his chimney pot blazing away. "I promise. I promise," he said. "*Please* put out the fire."

The fire officer smiled and turned on the water again. *SPLOOSH!* When the fire was out Mr Skinny Flint was so grateful, he invited the fire officer in for a cup of tea. A whole cup!

And from that day on, Mr Skinny Flint kept his promise and was never mean again.

11 A Big Sum

Two, add two elephants
That makes four -
Elephants in a row.
Add two more, to make it six
How many more to go?
Add three in a line - that makes nine
And one more, just for fun.
TEN clumping elephants on this page -
Now that's a VERY BIG SUM!

12 River Rescue

One day Noah was walking by the river in Noah's Park when he heard someone shouting. He looked along the riverbank and saw Mrs Rabbit waving her paws. She looked very worried. Noah hurried to see what was the matter.

"Look!" said Mrs Rabbit. "My babies have fallen in the water."

Noah looked and, sure enough, four baby rabbits were clinging to a log. They were being swept away downstream.

"We must stop them before they reach the waterfall," said Noah.

Just then two hippopotamus came ambling out of the wood. They were going to the river for a swim. "Please help us!" cried Noah. He pointed to the baby rabbits. The log was swirling faster and faster towards the waterfall.

The two hippos swam to the middle of the river as fast as they could. Then they turned back to back, and made a perfect dam right across the river. A moment later . . .

Bump! The log carrying the baby rabbits ran into them.

"Climb on our backs," said the hippos, "and hold on tight."

Very soon the baby rabbits were safely back with their mother, thanks to Noah and the two clever hippos.

13 Circles

The world is full of circles
Take a look and see,
All the rings and circle things
Surrounding you and me.

Cups and saucers
Plates and bowls
The iris in your eye;
The letter 'O'
A roundabout
The full moon in the sky.

A hoop to spin
A ring to wear
A record you can play;
Four rubber tyres
A steering wheel
To turn and drive away.

O o

The world is full of circles
So look around and say,
All the rings and circle things
You have found today.

14 Temper, Temper

Temper, temper Charlie Payne
In a tantrum, yet again.
Kicked the door and broke a chair
Pulled his sister, Sally's hair.
Snatched a picture off its hook
Tore the pages from a book.
Threw his toys around the place
Made a very ugly face.
Go to bed. Do as you're told.
Wake up, Charlie - good as gold.

15 Visiting Grandpa

Grandpa lives not far away
There are two ways we can go -
One way's through the village,
But the best way that I know
Is down along the riverbank
Where we can run and shout,
And look for silver fishes
As they swim and dart about.
Or walk across the footbridge
Where the river's flowing wide,
And wait to see whose stick boat
Floats out first the other side.

Grandpa says he doesn't mind
Whichever way we come.
He's always glad to see us
And visiting is FUN.

16 Special Delivery

It was a bright spring morning and Wormsley was delivering letters in Foxley Wood. Wormsley's post-bag was heavier than usual. It was Filbert Mouse's birthday on Saturday, and he had sent out lots of invitations to his party.

"I hope there's one for me," said Wormsley, as he sorted through a bundle of post.

There was an invitation for each of the rabbit children, Leafy, Flax and Berry. Mrs Longears was busy bathing them when Wormsley arrived.

"Thank you," said Mrs Longears taking the invitations in her soapy paw.

At Granny Fairweather's cottage there was a delicious smell of baking coming from the kitchen. Wormsley stood outside the window for a moment and had a good sniff.

"Come in," said Granny Fairweather. "I'm making cakes for Filbert's party."

"Goodness!" exclaimed Wormsley. "What a lot of cakes."

"I think Filbert has invited everyone in Foxley Wood," laughed Granny Fairweather. She handed Wormsley a newly-baked cake. "Here, have this for later."

Wormsley took the cake, thanked Granny Fairweather and went on his way. He wandered along the woodland path until he had delivered all the invitations. He looked in his bag, just to see if there was one for him at the bottom, but there wasn't.

"Filbert must have forgotten all about me," he said sadly.

On Saturday morning, Mrs Mouse was busy making sandwiches for the party. Filbert kept getting in her way. Mrs Mouse shooed him out of the kitchen.

"You can come and help me with the Treasure Hunt," said Mr Mouse.

They took a basket and dropped a trail of acorns along the woodland path. It was the same path that Wormsley had taken the day before.

Filbert was running ahead when he saw something lying on the ground. It was an envelope. And the envelope was addressed to - Wormsley.

"Look!" cried Filbert. "Wormsley's party invitation."

"We must deliver it at once," said Mr Mouse.

Filbert and his father hurried off to Wormsley's house, and knocked on the door.

"Special Delivery," said Filbert and handed him the invitation. Wormsley *was* surprised. He opened it and laughed.

"Fancy losing my own letter!" he said. "I must have dropped it on my way round."

So Wormsley went to Filbert's birthday party after all, and everyone had a wonderful time.

Breakfast Time

The juice in the mixer goes *wheee-wheee-whirr.*
The cereal in my bowl goes *crickle-crackle-snap!*
The milk from the jug goes *splish-sploosh-splosh.*
The bacon in the pan goes *sizzle-fizzle-splat!*
The bell on the cooker goes *ping-ting-a-ping.*
The coffee in the pot goes *puff-poddle-pop!*
My teeth on the toast go *crunch-crunch-crunch.*

And Daddy in the car goes *peep-beep-parp!*
"It's time to go to school."

Bouncing Baby Bill

Mrs Fidget's bouncy baby
Mother's little lamb,
Banged his rattle, sucked his toes
And jiggled in his pram.

One day Mrs Fidget's baby
Rolled out of the door.
Down the garden, through the hedge
To Mrs Brown next door.

Mrs Fidget's bouncing baby
Never could keep still.
So no one blamed her, when she named him
Bouncing Baby Bill.

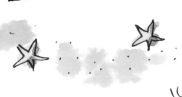

19 The Planet-Eating Giant

One day a huge spaceship landed on Planet Pongo. The door opened and out stepped an enormous giant. He was a planet-eating giant, and had come to see what Pongo tasted like. The giant looked around. There was no one in sight because the monsters who lived on Pongo were asleep. They sleep all day and wake up at night on Pongo.

The giant took a sniff. *Aaarh!*

"Pongo smells delicious," he said. The giant fetched a big bowl and a spoon from his spaceship. The spoon was the size of a shovel. He scooped up a lump of Pongo, and took a gigantic mouthful.

"Yum! Yum!" said the giant. "Pongo tastes like . . . er, let me see . . . strawberry jelly and custard!" So the giant ate a whole bowlful of Pongo. Then another, *and* another, until he was full up. At last the giant sat down. He was soon fast asleep and snoring loudly.

His snoring woke the little monsters, Meeny, Miny and Mo. They came running to see what was making all the noise. All their friends came too.

"Ooo!" cried Meeny. "A p-p-planet-eating giant."

"He's eaten lots already," said Miny.

"He'll eat us too!" wailed Mo.

Suddenly the giant woke up and saw all the little monsters staring at him. He got such a fright, he thought he was having a nightmare.

"Help!" shrieked the giant. "I must have eaten too much Pongo." He ran to the spaceship and took off with a *WHOOSH!*

"I don't think he'll come back again," said the little monsters.

And do you know? They were right.

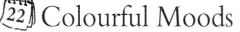

20 My Secret Monster

I know a secret cupboard
Where creepy crawlies hide.
And when I'm feeling very brave
I take a peep inside
To see the scary monster
With a hundred hairy legs,
And eyes the size of apple pies
In two enormous heads.
But should that monster see me
And turn his heads my way . . .
I'd shut that secret cupboard door
And run a mile away.

Very quickly.

22 Colourful Moods

When grown-ups say, "I'm feeling BLUE,"
It really means they're sad.
Or if they say, "I'm in the PINK,"
They're healthy, bright and glad.

It's strange the things that people say
Like, envy turns you GREEN.
Or someone's turned a ghostly WHITE
At frightening things they've seen.

It's odd the colours grown-ups go
Or *say* that they have been.
I stay the colour of my skin
Whatever mood I'm in.

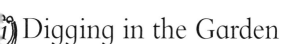

Digging in the Garden

Digging in the garden
Churning up the worms.
Clumps and clumps
Of sticky lumps
Rake them smooth in turns.

Now the soil is ready
To sow some tiny seeds.
Row by row
Of flowers grow
And in between . . . just weeds!

23 Washing

Washing on the clothes line
Drying in the sun.
Pyjamas, socks and dresses –
We peg them one by one.

Not long afterwards . . .

Listen! I hear thunder.
There it goes again.
Run and fetch the washing in
Before it starts to rain!

67

24 The Three Wishes

Once upon a time there was a poor fisherman called Jim Herring. His wife, Nancy, was always complaining about not having enough money to buy all the things they needed.

Early one morning, Jim was taking the fish he had caught to market.

"I'll be lucky if I can sell enough fish to buy a loaf of bread," said Jim.

Luckily for him, a good fairy overheard.

"I will grant you three wishes," she said. "Think carefully before you make each wish. Three are all you may have."

Well, Jim was so excited, he forgot all about going to market. He ran home to tell Nancy the good news. Nancy Herring danced a jig. There were so many things they wanted, she didn't know where to begin.

"Let's have breakfast, and decide what to wish for," she said.

Nancy put a pot of fish stew on the table.

"Oh no" said Jim. "Not stew *again*. I wish I could have a big fat sausage for breakfast." And, like magic, a big fat sausage appeared on his plate.

"You silly fishhead!" cried Nancy. "Look what you've done. You've wasted one whole wish."

Jim said he was sorry, but Nancy nagged him so much about the sausage that Jim lost his temper.

"I wish that sausage was stuck to your nose!" he shouted. The sausage stuck fast to Nancy's nose.

Nancy was furious.

"That's another wish gone," she yelled. Nancy tugged and pulled at the sausage, but it wouldn't come off.

"Don't just sit there," said Nancy. "Help me get this sausage off my nose."

Jim tried his best, but it wouldn't come unstuck.

At last Jim said, "We have one wish left. We must think very carefully what to wish for."

68

"Huh!" said Nancy. "There's only ONE thing to wish for. I wish this sausage would go away."

And it did. Just like that.

So Jim and Nancy were no better off than before. They had wasted those three wishes on one silly sausage. And even that had disappeared. What a pity!

Hunt the Guinea Pig

Round and round the garden
Everyone look for Fred.
We've got to find my guinea pig
Before I got to bed.

Mum says, "Mind my roses,"
Dad says, "Watch the cat.
If she finds Fred before we do . . .
That'll be the end of that."

Round and round the garden
We're all on hands and knees.
I *know* he's hiding somewhere -
Fred. Come out now, *please*!

Listen. I hear squeaking.
There! Behind the shed.
We all played hunt the guinea pig -
But I found Fred.

26 Fergus the Tractor

Fergus, the tractor, worked hard every day. He had a powerful engine for pulling and pushing every kind of farm machinery, to get all the jobs done.

One cold morning Malcolm, the farmer, came into the farmyard whistling. He gave Fergus a friendly pat on the bonnet.

"Wake up, Fergus," he said. "It's time to give the cows their breakfast."

Malcolm climbed into the cab. He sat in the seat and turned a key to start the engine. Fergus started up rightaway. Malcolm drove across the yard to where all the farm machinery was kept. He fixed a fork for lifting heavy bales of hay to the front of Fergus. Then he drove to the barn, where the hay was stored.

Inside the cab Malcolm pulled a lever. The fork lifted a giant bale high into the air, and Fergus carried it to where the cows were waiting to be fed. They were very hungry and mooed loudly when they saw him coming.

Malcolm pressed a pedal, and the fork lowered the bale and dropped it on to the ground. The cows munched away happily. After that Fergus went backwards and forwards to the barn for more hay, until there was enough to feed all those hungry cows.

"That's another good job done," said Malcolm, as he was driving Fergus back to the farmyard. "I can go and have my breakfast now!"

27 The Silly Billies and the Dragon

One day Mr and Mrs Goat took the billy kids up the mountain for a picnic. After lunch the billy kids wanted to explore on their own.

"Don't go too far," warned Mrs Goat.

"And mind the fierce old dragon who lives on the mountain," teased Mr Goat.

The billy kids scampered off up the path. In a while they came to a large cave.

"Ooo!" said the first billy kid. "I wonder if the dragon lives here?" The billy kids took one step inside the cave, when a voice boomed,

. . . *HERE - HERE - HERE.*

The billy kids jumped with fright.

"Quick!" said the other billy kid. "RUN!" As they raced down the mountainside they heard a voice calling after them,

. . . *RUN - RUN - RUN!*

The billy kids ran all the way back to their parents.

"There really *is* a dragon!" they said. "It lives in a cave and . . . ,"

"What did it look like?" asked Mr Goat, with a smile.

"Well, we didn't *see* it," said the billy kids. "But we *heard* it." Then they told their parents what had happened.

"You silly billies," said Mrs Goat. "What you heard was an ECHO." And they all laughed and went home.

28 The Old Coat

Katie kitten loved school. One day her teacher, Mrs Tabby said,

"We are going to do a play. It's all about wild animals."

Mrs Tabby asked everyone to think about what animal they would like to be. Katie knew straightaway.

"I'm going to be an elephant," she said.

"Good," said Mrs Tabby. Katie's friend, Tim, didn't know what he wanted to be.

"I'm sure you'll think of something," said Mrs Tabby.

When Katie got home, she told Ma Purrkins about the play.

"We'll have to make a costume," said Ma. "I've got just the thing for an elephant."

Ma Purrkins fetched an old grey coat that belonged to Pa.

"I've been meaning to take this to a jumble sale," said Ma. Katie put it on. Of course it was much too big.

"We could get two of you in there," said Ma. Katie thought of her friend, Tim and she had an idea.

"We could be an elephant together!" she said.

Katie took the coat to school next day, and Tim said he would love to be an elephant. The two friends bent over, and Mrs Tabby draped the coat across their backs. One sleeve dangled down at the front, just like a trunk.

"You'll have to practice trumpeting," said Mrs Tabby.

A week later Ma and Pa Purrkins went to see Katie's school play. When Katie and Tim took a bow, everyone clapped and cheered. Pa looked carefully at the elephant. "So *that's* where my old coat got to!" he said.

The Hare and the Tortoise

Once upon a time a fast-footed hare met a tortoise. They were on the road to a field full of ripe sweet corn. The tortoise was plodding along and looking forward to a feast of corn cobs.

The hare teased the tortoise for going so slowly.

"By the time you get there," said the hare, "the farmer will have harvested the corn and ploughed the field!" The tortoise smiled.

"Slow and steady, that's me," she said. "Still, I'm sure I could race you to the field."

The hare laughed his whiskers off. It seemed a ridiculous idea, but he agreed to have a race. A fox came to see them off.

"On your toes . . ." said the fox, "get set . . . go!"

The fast-footed hare dashed off, and left the tortoise far behind.

Now it was a sizzling hot day and soon the hare got tired from running. When he reached a river he stopped. He looked down the road and could just see the tortoise in the distance. Slowcoach! thought the hare. There's plenty of time for me to have a rest.

So he sat down by the bridge, and was soon fast asleep.

Meanwhile the tortoise was slowly catching up. The sun was warm on her shell, but she didn't stop. Not for a minute. And, while the hare went on sleeping . . . the tortoise caught up, and walked on over the bridge.

By the time the hare woke up, the tortoise was well ahead.

"How silly I've been!" said the hare. He was very cross with himself for stopping to rest, and ran as fast as his long legs could carry him.

But he was too late. When the hare got to the field, he found the tortoise there ahead of him.

"This sweet corn is delicious," said the tortoise with a grin.

"Oh, and by the way," she added. "I won the race. Slow and steady. That's me!"

30 Go to Sleep, Little Bear

Mr Bear is putting Little Bear to bed. When he has read three stories, Mr Bear closes the book, yawns and says,

"Now go to sleep, Little Bear."

"I'm not tired," says Little Bear.

"Here's your teddy," says Mr Bear.

"Read me another story," says Little Bear.

"Snuggle under the blankets," says Mr Bear.

"Just one."

"No," says Mr Bear. "Go to sleep."

"I'm wide awake," says Little Bear.

"Close your eyes," says Mr Bear. "Try counting sheep."

"I can't see any," says Little Bear.

"Try counting stars," says Mr Bear.

"Where?"

"There. Up there," says Mr Bear. "Look. We'll count them together. One . . . two . . . three . . . four . . . five . . . six . . ."

Mrs Bear comes in to say goodnight.

"Who's that snoring?" says Mrs Bear.

"Ssh!" says Little Bear. "Daddy's fast asleep!"

A Room with a Door and Not Much More

Miss Buttons lived all alone in a tiny house. It had a room with a door and not much more. One day a kangaroo hopped by her house.

"Can I live with you?" asked the kangaroo.

"I have a room with a door and not much more," said Miss Buttons, "but you are welcome to stay."

So the kangaroo moved in. Whenever Miss Buttons hung her washing on the line, the kangaroo carried the pegs in his pouch - which was helpful.

In a while a woolly sheep came by her house.

"Can I live with you?" asked the sheep.

"I have a kangaroo, a room with a door and not much more," said Miss Buttons, "but you are welcome to stay."

So the sheep moved in. Miss Buttons sheared the sheep, and knitted a warm jumper with the wool.

One afternoon it rained. The roof on the tiny house started to leak, and water *drip-drip-dripped* on the floor.

"Oh dear!" sighed Miss Buttons. Just then a pelican tapped his enormous beak on the window.

"Can I live with you?" asked the pelican.

"I have a sheep, a kangaroo, a room with a door and not much more," said Miss Buttons, "but you are welcome to stay."

So the pelican moved in. He stood where the water was dripping through the roof, and opened his beak like a bucket. It caught all the water, while Miss Buttons fixed the leak.

By now the tiny house was full up. What with the pelican, the sheep, and the kangaroo in a room with a door . . . there wasn't room for ANY more.

"We shall have to move," said Miss Buttons.

Now it happened that Miss Buttons had a friend called Ruby Cotton. She travelled around in a big caravan. As luck would have it, Ruby Cotton came to visit Miss Buttons the very next day.

"Can I live with you?" asked Miss Buttons.

"Of course!" said Ruby Cotton. "I've got plenty of room. And your friends can come too."

So Miss Buttons, the pelican, the sheep and the kangaroo all went travelling with Ruby Cotton.

And as for that tiny house? It has a room with a door and not much more - except for one little mouse family, who moved in last week.

1 Birthday Playtime

Monday's child plays doctors and nurses.

Tuesday's child reads silly verses.

Wednesday's child drives a racing car.

Thursday's child is a super star.

Friday's child is flying a jet.

Saturday's child is being a vet.

But Sunday's child just hasn't a clue
What in the world he's going to do.

2 Noisy Dora

Noisy Dora
What a snorer!
How her friends in town implored her,
"Noisy Dora, please don't snore,
We can't stand it any more."

Noisy Dora
Didn't care,
Turned her nose up in the air.
Caused a rumpus and a riot,
"Noisy Dora, do be QUIET!"

The last I heard
And, quite by chance
Noisy Dora went to France.
So if you go there, do make sure
Noisy Dora's not next-door.

New Chicks

Yellow chicks
Wobbly legs
Clamber out of
Crackly eggs.

Tiny beaks
Beady eyes
Fluffy feathers
Baby size.

Chirpy chicks
Little things
Huddle under
Speckled wings.

In the nest
Safe and warm
Mother keeps them
All from harm.

4 Who Lives Here?

"Knock, knock. Who lives here?
Who lives behind this door?"

Tyrannosaurus Rex. That's who.
The biggest dinosaur!
I'm heavier than an elephant
My jaws can open wide,
My teeth are sharp as daggers
So please, do step inside.
I feel a little peckish,
There's a rumbling in my tum . . .

"Some other time. But not today.
Right now I have to RUN!"

77

5 Grandma Tells a Story

Grandma was taking Jonathan to school one morning.

"I wish it wasn't such a long way," complained Jonathan.

"It's not far," said Grandma. "When I was your age it took me three hours to walk to school."

"Three *hours*," said Jonathan.

"Well . . . maybe two," said Grandma. "I had to get up at dawn and pack my things."

"What things?"

"Running shoes, climbing boots, torch, flippers . . . those kind of things," said Grandma.

"What for?"

"To get to school, of course," said Grandma.

She began her story.

"First I had to go by a farm, where there was a fierce bull in the field. He put his head down and charged at me every day. I had to run fast, I can tell you."

"I'm glad it wasn't me," said Jonathan.

"Then I had to climb a mountain," said Grandma. "Up one side and down the other. It was the only way."

"Wow!" said Jonathan.

"After that, there was the dark, spooky wood," said Grandma.

"Ooo!" said Jonathan. "Did you see any witches?"

"Lots," said Grandma. "One mean old witch cast a wicked spell, and turned me into a frog. I had to hop to school that day."

"Oh Grandma!" said Jonathan. "What next?"

"The last thing I had to do was swim across a shark-infested river," said Grandma.

"Sharks don't live in rivers," said Jonathan.

"They did in my day," said Grandma.

"Grandma," said Jonathan, "did you really, *really* do all those things?"

"Listen," said Grandma. "There goes the school bell."

"Grandma . . ."

"Run along," said Grandma. "I'll tell you later!"

6 Weather Reports

"The weather will be warm today,
Sunny, fine and bright."

I poked my head outside the door.
The weather man was right.

"The weather will be wet today,
With rainy April showers."

I put my new umbrella up
And walked about for hours.

"There's going to be a storm today,
With thunder claps and lightning."

I curled up with my cat and dog.
Thunder storms are frightening.

"The weather will be . . . *weathery* -
I'm not sure what to say."

Whatever the weather is going to do,
I'm going out to PLAY!

7 Busy Bees

One, two, three, four, five
Bumblebees around the hive
Taking nectar from each flower
Busy working hour by hour.

Six, seven, eight, nine, ten
Bumblebees fly home again
Dusting pollen from their knees
Busy buzzy bees.

8 Book Batty Nic

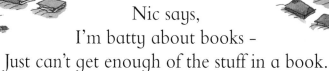

Nic says,
I'm batty about books -
Just can't get enough of the stuff in a book.

There are books about beetles, battles and trains,
Books about dinosaurs, football and drains.

There are books on computers, pirates and ships,
Books about dragons, fishes and chips.

I read something ghoulish to give me a fright,
There are volumes on vampires that bite in the night!

I pick up a joke book and have a good laugh,
With a flannel and soap, look I can read in the bath.

But the one that I'm reading's my favourite, you see
It's a book that tells everyone ALL ABOUT ME.

9 Golden Eggs

There was once a farmer's daughter called Dilly who was a bit of a dreamer. One morning her mother said,

"Go and collect the hens' eggs. Put them in this basket, and mind you don't break any."

So Dilly took the basket and wandered around the farmyard. As Dilly found each new-laid egg, she began to daydream.

"These aren't just any old eggs - they're made of gold! This golden egg will buy me the best silk dresses in town, with shoes to match."

Dilly smiled and popped another little egg in her basket. "With this golden egg I'll buy the finest coach and horses. Then a handsome prince will see me driving about, and invite me to the Ball."

Dilly imagined herself as a beautiful princess arriving at the palace, wearing a glittering ball gown. She had a diamond tiara which she had bought with yet another golden egg perched on top of her head.

Of course, the handsome Prince fell in love with Princess Dilly, and danced every dance with her. As they waltzed around the ballroom, Dilly whirled around the farmyard until . . . the basket flew out of her hand and all those eggs were smashed.

"There you go, daydreaming again!" said Dilly's mother. And, just like those eggs, poor Dilly's dreams went

CRACK-SPLATTER-SPLAT!

"Well it's nice to dream," said Dilly, "and one day a dream might come true."

 10 Mean Beans

11 Mrs Goosey Gander's Goslings

Mean Beans
Won't let me play
Say, "We don't want you.
Go away!"

Mean Beans
Whispering there
They've got a secret
I can't share.

Mean Beans
Play silly games
Hide my pencil case
Call me names.

Mean Beans
Picking on me
You'll be sorry,
You wait and see.
I've got a sister
Big and hairy.
When Jess gets angry,
She's really scary.

So, you'd BETTER WATCH OUT!

Mrs Goosey Gander's goslings
Off to have a swim
Flap and waddle to the lake –
SPLASH! They all jump in.

Mrs Goosey Gander's goslings
Follow in a line
Dip and paddle through the water –
One is far behind.

Mrs Goosey Gander's goslings
Swimming for the shore
Honk and scramble up the bank
Safely home once more.

12 The Wolf and the Five Baby Rabbits

Once upon a time a mother rabbit and her five babies lived together in a cottage by the meadow. And in the wood nearby lived a wolf, who was always hungry.

One morning Mother Rabbit said to her babies,

"I am going to the shops to buy a bunch of carrots. Stay inside the cottage, and don't open the door to anyone. It might be the wolf come to eat you up."

The five baby rabbits promised they wouldn't open the door, and Mother Rabbit went shopping.

She hadn't been away long, when there came a *tap-tap-tap* at the door. It was the wolf up to his tricks.

"Open the door," he said. "I've brought you a present."

The baby rabbits could just see two pointy ears outside the window.

"Go away," they said. "You're not our mother. She has long soft ears with smooth round tops."

So the wolf went away and thought of a cunning plan. He made himself a pair of long soft ears with smooth round tops, and stuck them on top of his head.

"I look just like Mother Rabbit now," he thought.

The wolf went back to the cottage and tapped at the door again.

"Open the door," he said. "I've brought you a present." The baby rabbits looked through the window. This time they saw two long soft ears with smooth round tops.

"It's our mother!" they shouted.

AND THEY OPENED THE DOOR.

The wolf sprang inside and bundled the terrified little rabbits into a sack - all except the youngest who had hidden under a chair.

The wicked wolf swung the sack over his shoulder and started for home. But the sack was heavy and, on the way, he stopped to rest. Soon he was fast asleep, dreaming of the fine rabbit pie he would have that night.

When Mother Rabbit got home and found all her babies gone, you can imagine how upset she was. Suddenly the youngest one crawled from his hiding place and told her what had happened.

"We must go after them at once," said Mother Rabbit.

As they ran along the path to the wood, Mother Rabbit paused, twitched her long soft ears with the smooth round tops and listened.

"I can hear snoring," she said. Soon they found the wolf still fast asleep, with the sack close by.

As quickly and as quietly as she could, Mother Rabbit untied the sack. Out hopped the baby rabbits – one, two, three and four.

"Now hurry!" whispered Mother Rabbit. "We must each find a big stone and put it in the sack."

So that is what they did. When the sack was full, Mother Rabbit tied it up and they all scampered home. At last the wolf woke up, and slung the sack on his back.

"Goodness!" chuckled the wolf, "this sack feels heavier than ever. I have caught the fattest little rabbits for my supper."

But when he got home and found that he had been tricked, the wolf was very angry. He howled with rage and threw the sack of stones in the air . . . and it came down and squashed him flat.

And from that day Mother Rabbit and her five babies lived happily for the rest of their lives.

13 Jacob's Ladder

Jacob Bun lived at number one, Acorn Avenue. One blowy day the wind blew the chimney off Jacob's roof. So Jacob fetched his ladder to fix it. He was working on the roof when . . .

Becky Blue at number two borrowed Jacob's ladder. She wanted to pick some apples from her apple tree. Becky Blue had climbed into the branches when . . .

Chris and Lea at number three borrowed Jacob's ladder. Their kite had landed on the garden shed. They were untangling the string when . . .

Angus More at number four borrowed Jacob's ladder to build a wall. Angus was laying the last few bricks along the top when . . .

Granny Chive at number five borrowed Jacob's ladder to clean her windows. Granny Chive had gone to get a bucket of water when . . .

Dudley Ricks at number six borrowed Jacob's ladder to reach his tree-house. He was holding a secret meeting with the gang when . . .

Mrs Devon at number seven borrowed Jacob's ladder to clip her hedge. She had finished trimming it when . . .

Mr Tate at number eight borrowed Jacob's ladder to paint his door. He was waiting for the paint to dry when . . .

Emily Fine at number nine borrowed Jacob's ladder to rescue her kitten. She had just brought kitty safely down when . . .

Gloria Gem at number ten gave a shriek. Bert, the burglar, had borrowed Jacob's ladder to steal Gloria's jewels.

Bert was climbing down the ladder with his loot when a policeman met him at the bottom.

"Come along," said the policeman. "Give Gloria back her jewels and say you are sorry. Then you can take this ladder back to where it belongs."

So Bert returned the jewels to Gloria Gem at number 10, and said he was sorry. Then he took the ladder back to Emily Fine at number 9. She took the ladder back to Mr Tate at number 8. He took the ladder back to Mrs Devon at number 7. She took the ladder back to Dudley Ricks at number 6. He took the ladder back to Granny Chive at number 5. She took the ladder back to Angus More at number 4. He took the ladder back to Sue and Lea at number 3. They took the ladder back to Becky Blue at number 2. And she popped next-door and took the ladder back to Jacob Bun at number 1.

Jacob had finished fixing his chimney and was wondering where his ladder had gone.

"Thank you for letting us borrow your ladder, Jacob," said everyone in Acorn Avenue.

"That's all right," said Jacob. "Only next time please . . . ASK ME FIRST!"

85

🗓14 The Teeny-Tiny Woman

Once upon a time there was a teeny-tiny woman who lived all by herself in a teeny-tiny house.

One day the teeny-tiny woman put on her teeny-tiny hat and went for a teeny-tiny walk. On the way she came to a teeny-tiny gate. The teeny-tiny woman opened the teeny-tiny gate and went into a teeny-tiny churchyard.

Now in the teeny-tiny churchyard there was a teeny-tiny bone. The teeny-tiny woman saw the teeny-tiny bone and said,

"This teeny-tiny bone will make some teeny-tiny soup for my supper."

So the teeny-tiny woman popped the teeny-tiny bone into her teeny-tiny pocket, and took it home to her teeny-tiny house.

By the time the teeny-tiny woman got home, she was feeling a teeny-tiny bit tired. She went upstairs to her teeny-tiny bedroom, and put the teeny-tiny bone into a teeny-tiny cupboard. Then the teeny-tiny woman lay on her teeny-tiny bed and fell asleep.

The teeny-tiny woman had been asleep for only a teeny-tiny time when she was woken by a teeny-tiny voice from the teeny-tiny cupboard. It said,

"Give me my bone!"

The teeny-tiny woman was a teeny-tiny bit frightened, so she hid under her teeny-tiny bedclothes and went to sleep again. And a teeny-tiny time later, the teeny-tiny voice cried out from the teeny-tiny cupboard a teeny-tiny bit louder,

"Give me my bone!"

This time the teeny-tiny woman was teeny-tiny more frightened. She put her teeny-tiny pillow right over her teeny-tiny ears and went to sleep again. But it was no good. In less than a teeny-tiny while that teeny-tiny voice shouted from the teeny-tiny cupboard,

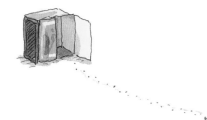

"Give me my bone!"

And because that teeny-tiny woman was frightened out of her teeny-tiny wits, she sat up in her teeny-tiny bed and said in her loudest, bravest teeny-tiny voice,

"TAKE IT!"

And that's the end of this teeny-tiny story.

15 Aristotle Humphrey Miller

Aristotle Humphrey Miller
Found a furry caterpillar,
Watched the caterpillar crawl
Through a crack and down a wall.
Followed it along the street
Dodging in and out of feet.
Till at last it reached a drain
Never to be seen again.
Said Aristotle Humphrey Miller,
"I really liked that caterpillar."

16 Sophie and the Mermaids

Sophie was learning to swim at school. Her teacher was very pleased with her.

"You'll be swimming like a mermaid soon," she told Sophie.

That night as Sophie lay in bed, she began to think what it would be like to be a mermaid. Dreamily she imagined herself gliding through the water with a fishy tail. As she swam, a voice whispered from her pillow,

"Left, right, hold on tight.
We're off to the Land of Dreams tonight."

It was Sophie's magic bed. All at once, it flew out of the bedroom window and, in less than a wink, they were over a blue ocean.

Sophie's bed turned itself into a boat and rocked gently on the waves. Sophie looked down into the crystal clear water and, suddenly she felt someone tugging her hair. It was a little mermaid.

"My name is Marina," said the mermaid."Come and see where I live."

With a flip of her tail, she dived into the depths below.

Sophie stood up in the bed boat, and jumped into the sea. She pulled herself through the water with her arms, kicking her legs, just as her swimming teacher had taught her. Down, down, down until . . .

her toes touched soft sand. She was standing on the bottom of the ocean. Marina beckoned and Sophie followed her to a coral cave. The roof was covered with the prettiest sea-shells Sophie had ever seen.

Sophie and Marina swam right inside the cave. It was full of mermaids! Some were playing hide-and-seek with brightly-coloured fishes that darted around the walls. But the most beautiful mermaid was sitting on a throne of pearls.

"That's the Mer-Queen," said Marina. "She is queen of all the mermaids."

The Mer-Queen turned and smiled at Sophie.

"Come here," she said. "I have a special gift for you."

She took a tiny pearl from her crown.

"Put this under your pillow," she said. "It will help you to swim - just like a mermaid."

Sophie thanked the Mer-Queen and clutched the tiny pearl in her hand.

"And now it is time to go," said Marina.

They swam back to the floating bed boat. Sophie said goodbye to Marina, and clambered on board… and arrived with a bump in the bedroom.

Sophie opened her eyes and saw her mum standing by the bed. She looked puzzled.

"Your hair is wet, Sophie," she said. "You must dry it properly next time you go swimming."

"I *thought* I had . . ." said Sophie.

When her mum had gone, Sophie looked under her pillow. There was the tiny pearl from the Mer-Queen's crown. Sophie jumped out of bed.

"I can't wait to go swimming again!" she said.

17 Half-Chick

There was once a hen who laid six beautiful eggs. When it was time for the chicks to hatch, six eggs cracked open but only five whole yellow chicks wobbled out. From the last, and smallest egg, came a half-chick.

He was a strange-looking bird with one wing, one leg and one beady eye. But for all Half-Chick had only half a head and half a beak, he had more to say for himself than all the other chicks put together. Half-Chick was also very selfish. From the minute he came into the world, he did just as he pleased.

One afternoon Half-Chick thought he would play a trick on his mother. He ran off and hid under a hedge. The poor hen spent hours calling him, afraid that he might be lost. When Half-Chick did come home that night, he pretended that he hadn't heard his mother calling, because he only had one ear!

As time went by, Half-Chick grew bored with life in the farmyard. He decided to leave home and go to the big city.

As he left the farmyard, his mother called after him,

"Half-Chick take good care of others, and others will care for you." But he pretended not to hear. After all, he had only one ear.

On the way to the city Half-Chick had to cross a stream. It was choked with weeds, so that the water could hardly flow at all. The water cried out to Half-Chick,

"Please help me by pulling up the weeds." But Half-Chick would do no such thing. And, since he had chosen not to hear his mother's good advice, he said rudely,

"Help yourself. I'm in a hurry to get to the city." He went on until he came to a cottage, which belonged to a farmer who was busy working in a field.

Now the farmer had left a pot of potatoes on the stove for his lunch. But the fire was nearly out and the potatoes were getting cold. So the fire shouted to Half-Chick,

"Please help me. Fetch some wood quickly!" But Half-Chick did no such thing. "Help yourself," he said. And he went on his way.

At last Half-Chick reached the city. What a place! he thought happily, as he hopped down a street. Just then a cook leaned out of his kitchen window, and grabbed Half-Chick by the neck.

"You'll make a tasty soup," said the cook. "Half a chicken is better than nothing." And he put Half-Chick in a pot of water over a fire.

"Oh help!" wailed Half-Chick. "Water, please don't boil. Fire, please don't burn. I don't want to be cooked."

The water said, "You didn't help me when I was a stream." The fire said, "You didn't help me when I needed wood."

And Half-Chick remembered his mother's good advice.

Take good care of others, and others will care for you.

But by then it was much too late.

 Nurse Jill

Nurse come quick!
Teddy's been sick
Dolly is looking quite pale.
Piggy's in bed with a very sore head
And Tiger's hurt his tail.

Nurse comes along
Sings them a song
Jokes and does the splits.
No need for a pill with nice Nurse Jill
She keeps the toys in fits!

 Little Bear Goes Shopping

Mr and Mrs Bear and Little Bear are shopping today.

First they go to the greengrocer's to buy some potatoes, a bunch of bananas and three large oranges.

"Can I carry them?" says Little Bear.

"Oh no," says Mr Bear. "You're much too small." And he puts the vegetables and fruit in a great big basket with red rope handles.

Next they go to the baker's shop to buy two crusty loaves, six sticky buns with icing on top and a currant cake.

"Can I carry them?" says Little Bear.

"Oh no," says Mrs Bear. "You're much too small." And she puts the bread, buns and cake into a middling-size basket on squeaky wheels.

As the three bears walk along the street, Little Bear feels sad. I'm too small to carry anything, he thinks. But just then, they come to a sweet shop.

"Ooo, yum, yum!" say the three bears. They go inside and buy a bag of humbugs for Mr Bear; toffees for Mrs Bear and, best of all, a big chocolate teddy for Little Bear.

"Can I carry them?" says Little Bear.

Mr Bear looks in his great big basket with red rope handles. It is full up. Mrs Bear looks in her middling-size basket on squeaky wheels. It is full up, too. But Little Bear has a tiny basket that is quite empty.

"YES PLEASE!" say Mr and Mrs Bear.

So Little Bear puts the humbugs, toffees and the big chocolate teddy in his tiny basket and carries them all the way home.

"What a good job you came shopping with us," say Mr and Mrs Bear. "We could never have managed without you, Little Bear!"

20 Owls

If owls are so clever
Why do they never
Sleep at night
Tucked up tight
In bed?

Why don't these brainy birds
Communicate to us in words
But choose to use
Tu-whit, tu whoos
Instead?

21 Three Pigs in a Tub

Rub-a-dub-dub
Three pigs in a tub
Scrubbing their trotters clean.
Snort, snout,
They all jump out
To roll in the mud again!

22 Birthday Balloons

Blowing up balloons
Takes a lot of puff,
Red, yellow, green and blue -
Have we got enough?

Huff and blow, up they go
Tie them in a knot.
Three balloons have flown away -
Fizzle. Bang. Pop!

Hang some in the window
And bunches round the room.
We'll give the Happy Birthday ones
To friends when they go home.

23 Surprise Washing

One morning Katie kitten was helping with the washing.
Ma Purrkins filled a big basket with wet clothes to be hung
out to dry. There was more than usual today.

Pa Purrkins was helping too.

"I'll carry the basket," he said.

"And I'll help peg the clothes on the line," said Katie.

Katie took the peg bag into the garden, and handed Pa some pegs. They hung out; pyjamas, trousers,
three woolly jumpers and a shirt.

"Those are all my things," said Pa.

Then Katie helped Pa to hang up a skirt, blouse and nightgown belonging to Ma.

"Any more?" asked Pa with a smile.

When Katie looked in the basket she got quite a surprise. Right at the bottom was a tiny dress, socks,
vest and pants.

"These *look* like mine," said Katie, "but they're much too small."

"Oh dear!" said Pa. "They must have shrunk in the wash."

Katie ran inside to tell Ma Purrkins what had happened.

"All my clothes have shrunk!" cried Katie.

Ma Purrkins laughed.

"They weren't *your* clothes," she said. "They belong to an
old rag doll of mine. I thought I would wash her clothes and
brush her hair and . . . give her to someone special."

Just for a moment Katie looked sad.

"Who?" she asked.

"Why, YOU of course!" said Ma.

24 A Little Monkey

I,
Sing like a bird

Swim like a fish

Kick like a donkey

Run like a hare

Eat like a pig

Sleep like a sloth

Leap like a frog

Climb like a bear

And sometimes . . . I'm just a little monkey.

25 All in a Row

Shops in a street,
Bricks in a wall,
Trees in the forest
Straight and tall.

Peas in a pod
Packed in tight;
Keys on a piano
Black and white.

Teeth of a crocodile,
Birds on a wire,
Children in assembly
Singing in a choir.

Desks in the classroom,
Books on a shelf . . .
Think of all the rows you know
And write them down yourself!

95

26 Bernard the Bulldozer

Bernard, the bulldozer, was one of the strongest machines around. His mighty engine was very powerful. He could push rocks and earth away with the huge blade on his front. And instead of wheels, Bernard had two steel crawler tracks. He could move over the muddiest ground without ever getting stuck.

One April morning Bernard and his driver, Bob, were clearing the way for a new road. Bernard had just scooped up a mound of earth when Bob saw something moving in it.

"What have we got here, Bernard?" said Bob peering through the cab window.

It was a frog. Bob looked more closely and saw another frog scrambling over the soil. And another. He was sure a whole family of frogs had been caught up in the load.

"We must take these frogs to safety, Bernard," said Bob.

Bob looked around until he spotted a pond. It was well away from where the new road was to be built. So Bob worked the controls and Bernard crawled over the muddy field. He carefully carried that great mound of earth towards the pond, with the frogs sitting on top.

When they were near the bank, Bob said, "That's far enough."
Bernard stopped, and the frogs hopped off to find a new home.

"And now, Bernard," said Bob, "we must get back to work on that new road!"

27 Be Brave, Potter Pig!

One day Potter Pig was trying out his new bicycle. Round the garden, faster and faster until,

"Help!" cried Potter. "I can't stop."

He bumped into a wall, fell off and cut his knee.

Mrs Pig picked him up and gave him a cuddle. "Let's go and put a big plaster on your poor knee," she said.

Later Potter showed his wounded knee to his friends.

"I had to have a really BIG plaster," he told them.

Soon Potter's knee was better.

"Time to take that old plaster off," said Mrs Pig. Potter looked worried. The plaster was stuck tight to the little hairs on his leg.

EXTRA BIG
Plasters
for nasty cuts
very sticky

"I'll do it," he said. But he didn't.

"Come along," said Mrs Pig. "I'll pull it off for you."

"No!" said Potter.

"After three," said Mrs Pig stooping down. "One . . ."

"Don't touch it!" said Potter.

"Be brave," said Mrs Pig. "Two."

"Please!" said Potter.

"I'll give you a chocolate biscuit," promised his mum. "Three!"
And she pulled the plaster OFF.

"There," said Mrs Pig, "all done." Potter looked at his knee.

"I was brave, wasn't I?" said Potter.

"Yes," said his mum opening the biscuit tin. "You were!"

28 A Piece of Nothing

There was once a dog who went to market, to see what he could find. His nose went *sniff-snuffle-snuff* and soon, he had sniffed his way to a butcher's stall.

The butcher was busy with customers. He didn't see the dog lurking nearby. Then suddenly, *sniff-snaffle-snap!* The greedy dog snatched a big piece of meat off the slab.

"Stop!" cried the butcher. But he was too late. The dog had run off down the road.

The dog was very pleased with himself. He ran flat out until he came to a river. There was a little bridge over the water and, on the other side, the dog could see a clump of bushes. I'll hide under those bushes, he thought, and eat my meal in peace.

So the dog started to cross the bridge, *pit-patter-pad*. But halfway across, he happened to look down into the water. It was deep and dark and still.

And there, staring back at him from the river, there appeared to be another dog – just like himself – with a big piece of meat in its mouth. The greedy dog could hardly believe his eyes. I'll have that meat too, he thought.

The greedy dog opened his jaws to snatch it and . . . *SPLASH!* He dropped his own meat in the river. It sank to the bottom of the muddy water and was gone. Now, instead of having two meals, he had none.

A fish popped its head out of the water and laughed.

"Serves you right for being so greedy," said the fish. And the dog had to agree he was right.

 29 Whose Egg is This?

One Spring afternoon Noah found a strange new egg in the Park. It was a very big egg, and Noah wondered who it could belong to.

First he went to see Mrs Turtle.

"Have you lost an egg?" asked Noah.

Mrs Turtle crawled along to look at the egg.

"No," she said. "It's not mine."

In a while Mr and Mrs Emu came running along. Noah asked them about the egg, too.

Mr and Mrs Emu peered at the egg and shook their heads.

"It's not ours," they said.

After that Noah went down to the river. He found Mrs Alligator basking in the sun.

"Have you lost an egg?" asked Noah.

Mrs Alligator thought for a moment. She couldn't be sure if she had lost one or not, so she hurried along with Noah to have a look at it.

"No," said Mrs Alligator. "It's not mine."

Just then Noah heard something large crashing through the trees. It was an enormous dinosaur, with a long swishy tail.

"HAS ANYONE SEEN MY EGG?" boomed the dinosaur. It was Mrs Stegosaurus and she looked very worried.

Noah pointed to the egg. "Is this yours?" he asked.

Mrs Stegosaurus took one look at the egg and said, "Yes, that's MINE. I left it in my nest for just a moment, but it must have rolled away."

Mrs Stegosaurus thanked Noah for finding her egg.

"Well," said Noah, "if it ever rolls away again, I'll know who it belongs to."

30 Lost and Found

Doctor Dog is cross with himself this morning. He has lost his glasses *again*. He can't remember where he put them down.

"You're always losing your glasses," says Nurse Kitty.

Doctor Dog is still looking for them when Mrs Elephant comes into the surgery.

"Do sit down," says Doctor Dog. And he tells Mrs Elephant about his glasses.

"That's funny," says Mrs Elephant, "I'm sure I remember seeing your glasses on a chair . . ."

"Oh no!" says Nurse Kitty. "I think I know which one. Would you mind standing up again please, Mrs Elephant."

Mrs Elephant stands up and *there* are Doctor Dog's glasses. Mrs Elephant has sat on them, and they have been squashed flat. She looks very upset.

"Never mind," says Doctor Dog. "I needed a new pair of glasses. And it *was* a silly place to leave them."

Then Mrs Elephant tells Doctor Dog why she has come to see him.

"I keep forgetting things," she says.

"Well," says Doctor Dog, "we all forget things sometimes. But you remembered where you had seen my glasses."

"I've got an idea that will help you both," says Nurse Kitty.

She goes to a cupboard and takes out two new handkerchiefs, and gives one each to Doctor Dog and Mrs Elephant.

"Next time you want to remember something," says Nurse Kitty, "just tie a knot in your handkerchief."

And it worked. Well, almost. Now Doctor Dog always knows where his glasses are - but he keeps on losing the hanky!

1 Hilda's New Broomstick

One morning Alfred Jones went to see his friend, Hilda Brimstone who lived on the top floor of Moonshine Mansions. Hilda was a witch and she and Alfred got on very well.

On this particular morning, however, Hilda looked a bit disappointed to find Alfred at the door.

"I thought you were my new broomstick," she said.

"I'm afraid not," said Alfred.

"Come in anyway," said Hilda. "You can help me try it out, when it arrives."

"Thank you," said Alfred.

Hilda told Alfred all about her new broomstick.

"It's the latest thing," she said. "I chose it from a Mail Order catalogue." She opened the catalogue at a page full of broomsticks.

"That one," said Hilda pointing to the biggest.

Alfred read the description.

"*High-speed Zoom Broom. Fully automatic broomstick for fast, trouble-free flying, with a built-in computerised homing device.*"

"What's the homing thing?" asked Hilda's cat, Hubble.

"It helps the broomstick find its way home," said Hilda.

As she spoke there was a terrible crash outside Moonshine Mansions, followed by the tinkling sound of broken glass. A high-speed, fully automatic Zoom Broom, with a built-in computerised homing device had just crashed through Matthew Plummer's bedroom window, on the second floor.

Alfred, Hilda and Hubble rushed downstairs and found Matthew examining the broomstick excitedly. Matthew was Alfred's friend and a genius with computers.

"I'll just re-programme the homing device for you," he said. "Then it will work perfectly."

"Thank you," said Hilda. "I'm not much good with these new-fangled inventions. But I can fix your window with a bit of magic." She muttered a spell and clicked her fingers – snap! And Matthew's window was as good as new.

When Matthew had fixed the homing device Alfred said,

"Can we take the Zoom Broom for a test flight now?"

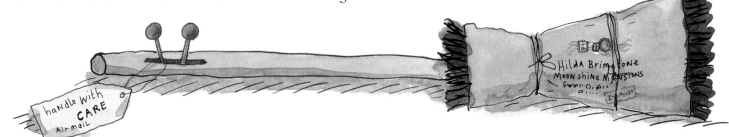

"Yes," said Hilda, "and Matthew can come too."

So they all sat on the broomstick, with Hubble clinging on behind.

"Goodness knows where we'll end up," he muttered. Hubble didn't trust the new broomstick at all.

"Ready?" said Hilda.

"Full power," said Alfred.

"Go!" said Matthew.

And they flew out of the room, and up round the chimney pots all afternoon.

At teatime Alfred tried to tell his mother about the new broomstick.

"Oh yes," said Mrs Jones, who didn't believe Alfred for a minute.

"And I suppose the witch's cat was flying around with you?"

"Well," said Alfred, "as a matter of fact, he WAS!"

 ## 2 All About Me

I've got . . .

A head for nodding, shaking and thinking,
Eyes for seeing, closing and blinking.

Ears for hearing nice things and boring,
A nose for smelling, blowing and snoring.

A mouth for speaking, eating and kissing,
Teeth for chewing - my front tooth is missing.

Arms for waving, hugging and squeezing,
Hands for clapping, helping and pleasing.

Elbows and knees for bending and stretching,
Legs for kicking, running and fetching.

And right at the bottom my two little feet
For dancing and tapping a musical beat.

3 Katie and Mrs Duck

One evening Ma and Pa Purrkins were going out for a little while, and Mrs Duck had come to look after Katie kitten.

Ma and Pa kissed Katie goodbye.

"I don't want you to go," said Katie.

"We won't be long," said Ma.

"Be good," said Pa.

"We'll have some fun," said Mrs Duck.

As Ma and Pa closed the door, Katie began to cry.

"I can do magic tricks," said Mrs Duck pulling six silk handkerchiefs from under her wing.

"I don't like magic tricks," sniffed Katie. But secretly she did.

Next Mrs Duck balanced some bouncing balls on her beak. Katie stopped crying.

"Can I have a go?" she asked. Katie tried to balance a ball on her nose, but it wobbled off.

When they had played for a while, Mrs Duck said, "It's bathtime, Katie."

"Can't we play a *little* longer?" said Katie.

"We can play in the bath," said Mrs Duck.

So they went to the bathroom and Mrs Duck turned on the taps. *SWOOSH!* went the water.

"Here's the bubble stuff," said Katie. Mrs Duck squirted in lots and lots. There were bubbles everywhere.

Then Katie climbed into the bath, and Mrs Duck jumped in after her. *SPLASH!* She paddled up and down in the soapy foam which made Katie laugh.

The two were having such a good time, they didn't hear Ma and Pa Purrkins come home. Ma popped her head round the bathroom door.

"What's all this noise?" she said with a smile. Some bubbles floated out through the door on to the landing.

"And what's all this mess?" said Pa.

Later, when Mrs Duck had gone and Katie was tucked up in bed, Ma and Pa came to say goodnight.

"Will Mrs Duck be coming again?" asked Katie.

"Next time we go out," said Ma.

"If you want her to," said Pa.

"Yes," said Katie. "I do."

Fairy Mary

Mary was a fairy with a swishy, wishy wand,
But clumsy Fairy Mary dropped her wand in a pond.
Now Fairy Mary's fishing for her *fishy* wishy wand!

The Skeleton of Henry Jones

The skeleton of Henry Jones
Is just a lot of funny bones.
A skull, some teeth and in between
Two sockets where his eyes have been.
It hasn't any skin or hair,
No crinkly wrinkles anywhere.

What was he like?
We'll never know.
He lived two hundred years ago!

6 Time For Bed

It's time for bed,
Daddy said,
Now put your toys away.
Up the stairs
To say your prayers,
No "buts", do as I say.

Brush your hair,
Clean your teeth,
We'll read some stories too.
Then count some sheep
And off to sleep,
The rascally pair of you!

7 The Chase

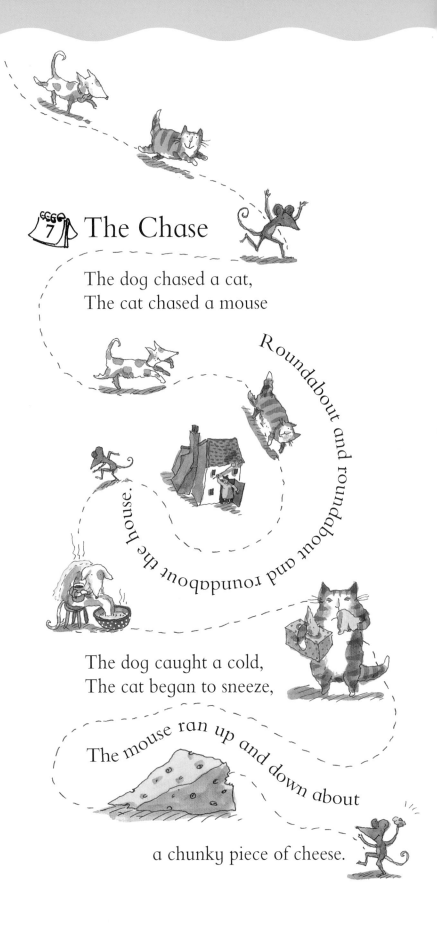

The dog chased a cat,
The cat chased a mouse

Roundabout and roundabout and roundabout the house.

The dog caught a cold,
The cat began to sneeze,

The mouse ran up and down about

a chunky piece of cheese.

8 All Year Bears

January bears sleep in lairs

February bears sit on chairs

March bears run like hares

April bears walk in pairs

May bears stand and stare

June bears fly in the air

July bears wash their ears

August bears have no cares

September bears pick ripe pears

October bears climb the stairs

November bears love city squares

December bears live . . . anywheres!

9 Thing-a-Me Bob and the Blob of Blubber

There was once a man called Thing-a-Me Bob, who lived in a shack by the sea. Thing-a-Me Bob spent his days making up names for everything around him, which he thought was very clever.

He called his shack, 'crusty pie',

the beach, 'shilly-shally-shelly-o',

and the wide blue sea, 'wavy gravy'.

Now one day there was a terrible storm. The wind blew and the waves rose up, high as mountains. Thing-a-Me Bob looked out of his window and saw a gigantic whale, tossing about in the sea. It was very close to the beach and his shack.

"Oh no!" cried Thing-a-Me Bob. "A blob of blubber".

Thing-a-Me Bob telephoned the Coast Guard for help.

"Come quickly!" he shouted. "There's a blob of blubber in the wavy gravy, right by the shilly-shally-shelly-o, and it's heading for my crusty pie."

Well, the Coast Guard couldn't understand a word Thing-a-Me Bob was saying. She thought the funny man was playing a joke, so she put the phone down.

Then the blob of blubber ate up the crusty pie, Thing-a-Me Bob and all. *Snip! Snap!*

And that was that.

10 Follow-my-leader

We're playing Follow-my-leader,
Everyone get in line.
Quick march! Left, right, left, right, left, right -
Try to keep in time.

We're playing Follow-my-leader,
Everyone make a chain.
Chuff chuff, choo choo, wah wah, wooo wooo!
Just like a puffer train.

We're playing Follow-my-leader,
Everyone round the park.
Two by two by two by two,
Animals into the ark!

11 Play in May

Girls and boys come out in May,
Bring your friends to the park and play.

Race you all to the climbing frame,
Up the ladder and down again.

Hold on tight to the roundabout,
It spins so fast, we scream and shout.

"Push me high on the swing," says Sue,
She's trying to touch the sky with her shoe.

"One last go on the slide," says Mum.
"I've got to get my shopping done!"

12 The Clay Baby

Daisy Bloom was a potter. Her house was full of pots, bowls and jugs she had made. One Monday morning Daisy was busy in her pottery. She threw a lump of soft buttery clay on the wheel. It oozed through her fingers and dribbled down her elbows.

Daisy pedalled the wheel to make it spin. Soon it was whirling round at a fierce rate, and Daisy had to hold on tight to the slippery lump. But on this particular morning, something extraordinary happened.

The lump wriggled and squiggled and hurled itself to the floor. One tiny piece broke off and rolled into a corner. The big lump jumped up and hid behind some pots. Only it wasn't a lump. It was a clay baby.

"Catch me if you can," he giggled.

Daisy was as pleased as anything.

"I've always wanted a *real* baby," she said. "But this one will do just as well."

Daisy caught the baby and showed him to her husband, Stanley.

"What a lovely baby," he said.

On Tuesday Stanley took the clay baby shopping. When they got to the supermarket, the baby skipped away and found a trolley. The trolley made a good racing car.

"*Vroom!*" went the runaway baby. He sped by the baked beans, and crashed into some fresh cream cakes.

Stanley grabbed the baby and pulled him out of the mess.

"*I'll* push the trolley, next time," said Stanley sternly.

Every day that week the clay baby got into mischief. On Sunday, while they were having a picnic in the country, he was really naughty. He ran into a field and chased some sheep.

"*Shoo! Shoo!*" he laughed.

"*Baa! Baa!*" cried the worried sheep with their lambs. The farmer was very angry.

That evening Daisy sent the clay baby to bed without any supper.

She wondered if he would EVER behave. It was as if a little piece of good was missing. And that set Daisy thinking. She thought about the day the clay baby had been made, and remembered how one tiny piece of clay had broken off and rolled into the corner.

Daisy hurried to the pottery and searched for that tiny piece of clay. At last she found it, picked it up and looked at it carefully.

"Just as I thought," she said. "It's full of goodness!"

So Daisy took that tiny lump of goodness to the sleeping baby, and pressed it over his heart. And from then on, things were quite different. The clay baby was as good as he could be, and naughty sometimes - just like a real baby.

13 Saturday Sweets

Creamy eggs,

Sugar mice,

Chewy toffee bars;

Liquorice loops,

Chocolate chips,

Fizzy sherbet stars.

Gummy snakes and

Dinosaurs,

Lollies on a stick,

We eat them all on Saturday
And Sunday - we feel sick!

Easy-peasey-pie!

Once upon a time there was a mean old dog and a cat called Puss and they were always fighting. One day the dog bit Puss's ear off.

"Give me my ear," says Puss.

"No," says the dog. "Go to the butcher and fetch me a bone. Then I'll give you your ear."

"Easy-peasey-pie," says Puss.

So off she went with a skip and a hop,
'Til she came at last to the butcher's shop.

"Please give me a bone," says Puss to the butcher. "I'll give the bone to the dog, and the dog will give me my ear again."

"No," says the butcher. "Go to the baker and fetch me a cake. Then I'll give you a bone."

"Easy-peasey-pie," says Puss.

So off she went with a skip and a hop,
'Til she came at last to the baker's shop.

"Please give me a cake," says Puss to the baker. "I'll give the cake to the butcher, the butcher will give me a bone, I'll give the bone to the dog, and the dog will give me my ear again."

"No," says the baker. "Go to the grocer and fetch me a cheese. Then I'll give you a cake."

"Easy-peasey-pie," says Puss.

So off she went with a skip and a hop,
'Til she came at last to the grocer's shop.

"Please give me a cheese," says Puss to the grocer. "I'll give the cheese to the baker, the baker will give me a cake, I'll give the cake to the butcher, the butcher will give me a bone, I'll give the bone to the dog, and the dog will give me my ear again."

"No," says the grocer. "Go to the fishmonger and fetch me a fish. Then I'll give you a cheese."

"Easy-peasey-pie," says Puss.

So off she went with a skip and a hop,
'Til she came at last to the fishmonger's shop.

The fish smelled delicious.

"Please give me a fish," says Puss to the fishmonger, licking her lips. The kind fishmonger looked at the one-eared cat and said,

"YES!" And gave Puss the biggest, fattest fish she had ever seen.

Puss thought about the grocer, the baker, the butcher and the mean old dog for a moment. Then she said,

"I'll make do with one ear from now on!" And she ate that great big fish all by herself.

"Easy-peasey-pie!" says One-Eared Puss.

15 The Last Gingerbread Man

When I was passing the baker's shop,
I saw something that made me stop.
A gingerbread man, all by himself
Flat on his back, on the window shelf.
He was gingery brown from his head to his toes,
With two curranty eyes and a nut for a nose.
And something about him seemed to say,
"Please, will you buy me and take me away?"

So I bought the very last gingerbread man . . .
Now I'm eating him up as fast as I can!

16 Ruff, Gruff and Billy

Ruff, Gruff and Billy were three little goats who ate *everything*. Matty, the farmer, did her best to stop them eating things they shouldn't touch.

They ate the horse's oats.

They munched the flowers in Matty's garden.

Once they chewed the clothes on her washing line!

Now one moonlit night Ruff, Gruff and Billy got into a field of cabbages. Matty *was* to have taken the cabbages to market the next day. Ruff, Gruff and Billy were having a lovely time nipping off the leaves until Matty came out of the farmhouse and saw them.

"Off! Shoo! Go away!" cried Matty, rushing after them and waving a stick. The goats took no notice.

Matty's cries woke the sheepdog in his kennel. He chased the goats round the field too. But the sheepdog couldn't catch them. Ruff, Gruff and Billy hopped round those cabbages, quick as anything.

Matty sat down and cried. All the cabbages were ruined. She would have nothing to sell at market.

"Enough is enough!" Matty said to Ruff, Gruff and Billy. Then, first thing in the morning, she marched those goats off to market and sold them for a very good price.

17 Small Things

Apple pips, a drop of rain;
One button off my coat *again*.

Birthday candles, purple plums;
Two pink plasters on my thumbs.

Ladybirds and crawling snails;
Three little pigs with curly tails.

A tray of tarts, my favourite cup;
Four little puddles from a new-born pup.

Butterflies and grains of sand;
Five finger puppets on my hand.

Cotton reels, seashore shells;
Six bats swinging from old church bells.

Blobs of paint, dotty spots;
Seven birds perched on chimney pots.

House door keys, a fairy ring;
Eight sweet notes that I can sing.
(doh-ray-me-fa-so-la-te-doh)

Mewing kittens, flower seeds;
Nine bright wooden necklace beads.

Postage stamps, my bucket and spade;
Ten toy bandsmen on parade!

18 The Nimble Weaver

Little spider on a thread
Spinning at your sticky web,
Silently you wind each strand,
Weave it to a pattern planned.
Nimble weaver,
Hear me sigh –
All that work to catch a fly!

19 Mrs Platt Made a Hat

Mrs Platt made a hat
Dressed it up with this and that;
Fruit and berries round the brim,
Ribbons for her double chin,
Cherry blossom on the crown,
Feathers from an eiderdown.
She wore it walking down the street –
Thought she looked a proper treat.
Until two sparrows perched to rest,
Settled down and built a nest.

Now Mrs Platt prefers to wear,
The latest bird's nest in her hair.

113

20 Mud

There's a muddy little puddle
By the duckpond on our farm,
With squeedgy, squidgy mud in it
That trickles down my arm.
It squelchs through my fingers,
And in between my toes;
I can't think how it happens
But mud gets up my nose.
My hair has sludgy lumps of it,
It splatters round my eyes . . .
There's always loads of mud on ME
When I make my mud pies.

21 The Way to School

Down the garden,
Through the gate,
Along the road,
At half-past-eight.
Round the corner,
Up the street,
Here comes Amy,
Max and Pete.
Right at the station,
Left by the shops,
Cross the road
When the traffic stops.
The school bell clangs.
The clock strikes nine . . .
Run to the playground,
Just in time!

our House
AMY
station
Max
Pete
shops
Me
our school
playground
Lots of traffic

22 Things People Do

Farmers grow the crops we eat,

Bakers make us bread,

Fisher folk go out to sea

While we are warm in bed.

Authors write the books we read,

Artists paint and draw,

Photographers take photographs,

Policemen keep the law.

Teachers help us learn at school,

Doctors make us well,

Workers in a factory

Make things to buy and sell.

An astronaut in Outer Space,

A keeper in the zoo,

When you grow up, what will you be?

There's SOMETHING you can do!

23) The Missing Stripes

Doctor Dog and Nurse Kitty are out visiting some patients today. First they visit Nigel Worm.

"Please come out of your hole," says Doctor Dog.

"I can't," says Nigel. "I'm stuck."

So Doctor Dog and Nurse Kitty pull him out and, after a few squirms, Nigel feels much better.

After that they go and see Stripy Tiger. He says he has lost some stripes. Doctor Dog examines him carefully. One side is very stripy. The other side is not.

"Dear me," says Doctor Dog. "I wonder where your stripes have gone?"

Then Nurse Kitty notices a muddy patch where Stripy Tiger has been lying. She opens her First Aid box and takes out a hair brush.

"I think I know where your stripes have gone," says Nurse Kitty.

She gives Stripy Tiger's coat a good brush – and THERE are his stripes underneath all the mud.

"Your missing stripes were there all the time," laugh Doctor Dog and Nurse Kitty.

And they hurry off to visit all the other patients.

24)  Something Awful

I found something awful on the refrigerator shelf.
I'd say it had been there for a week, or more.
But yesterday, all by itself
It flopped on the floor - *Kerplup!*
And our dog, Digger lapped it up.
Slup, slup, slup!

He thought that awful something was scrumptious.

115

25 Hidden Treasure

There was once a farmer who had two sons called Rick and Davy. Every day they worked hard in the fields. The soil was rich and their crops grew well. But there came a day when the farmer was too old and weak to work, so he called his sons to his bedside.

"I am going to tell you a secret," he said. "There is treasure on this farm. It's yours if you take the trouble to look for it. As soon as the harvest is over, dig the fields again and again. Then, sow corn seed ready for next spring." Rick and Davy's eyes opened wide with excitement at the thought of finding treasure.

Soon afterwards the old man died and his sons got to work. They harvested the crops and stored them in the barn. Then they busied themselves digging in the fields. Clod by clod they dug deep into the earth, searching for that treasure. But they couldn't find a thing.

"Keep digging!" said Rick.

"It must be here somewhere," said Davy.

Rick and Davy dug every part of land and sowed more crops, just as their father had said. When spring came round again, their fields were full of lush green corn. The corn ripened in the summer sun and, at harvest time, they gathered in twice as much as before. Rick and Davy stored all they needed, and sold the rest at market. They came home, their pockets bulging with coins.

"Now I'm beginning to see what Dad meant about treasure," said Rick. "The 'treasure' is our reward for working hard on the farm."

"Yes," said Davy, "trust Dad to make work sound like a treasure hunt!"

But they both agreed it was good advice.

The Whistle

One sunny afternoon in May Hee Haw Donkey and Humpy Camel were walking near the Tum Tum tree. The sun shone through the branches and sparkled on something shiny, lying on the path. It was a silver whistle.

"What's this?" said Hee Haw Donkey. "I wonder if it growls?" He tapped it with his hoof, but it didn't growl.

"Does it bite?" said Humpy Camel. He peered at it carefully, but it didn't bite.

They were still looking at it when Giraffe With a Scarf came by. He bent down and said,

"Does it hop?" Giraffe With a Scarf stamped his foot, but the whistle didn't hop.

Just then Police Constable Fox came hurrying along. He seemed to have lost something.

"Has anyone seen my whistle?" he asked.

"Is this it?" said Hee Haw Donkey. "It doesn't growl."

"It doesn't bite," said Humpy Camel.

"And it doesn't hop," said Giraffe With a Scarf.

Police Constable Fox picked up his whistle and laughed.

"No," he said, "it doesn't do any of those things." He put the whistle to his mouth and . . . blew it.

whoooo-eeee!

"So THAT's what it does!" they all said.

27 Fine Feathers

Parrot, Pelican and Peacock were sitting in an oak tree arguing. The three couldn't agree who was the best bird amongst them.

"It must be me," screeched Parrot. "I have the brightest feathers."

"Nonsense," said Pelican. "Look at my magnificent beak. It's bigger and better than yours."

"Your beak and your feathers are nothing compared to my tail!" boasted Peacock. He strutted up and down, spreading out his spectacular tail in a fan – which was very beautiful.

All this time the oak tree said nothing, but it thought the birds were vain and foolish.

While they were quarrelling, another bird came along. It was Crow in disguise. Crow thought her own feathers were dull. So she had collected as many different kinds of feathers as she could find, and had stuck them on her wings. Parrot, Pelican and Peacock had never seen another bird quite like her before. They agreed she was the best of them all.

The oak tree rustled its leaves. Fine feathers do not always make a fine bird, it thought. Besides, each one of those silly birds is beautiful in its own way.

Hattie and Jake

Hattie and Jake were hunting – or rather, Hattie was hunting and Jake was hoping to share anything Hattie might catch.

Hattie twitched her long whiskers and crept forward. She crouched, quivered and pounced.

"Got you!" growled Hattie through a mouth full of mouse.

I wish I was a good mouser, thought Jake, as he watched Hattie run off with her prize.

Jake wandered into the kitchen. *Sniff. Sniff.* Jake could smell something good. His owner, Jane, was cutting fruit. Melon! Jake loved melon almost as much as mice. But he didn't have to hunt for it. Jane threw him a piece of fruit and Jake caught it in mid-air.

"Got you!" purred Jake happily, chewing up the rind.

Later, when Jake heard Hattie coming home, he ran and hid behind the kitchen door. Jake crouched, quivered and pounced – just like a real hunter. The two cats tumbled together in a furry ball pretending to be fierce tigers until Hattie held Jake's head firmly between her paws . . . and began to wash his ears!

Then the two friends purred and washed and purred themselves to sleep.

29 Noah's Garden

It was a fine day and Noah decided to do some gardening. He looked at his lawn. The grass had grown so much, it was almost up to his knees. Noah fetched his lawn mower and got to work. *Clutter-clutter-clutter-clutter-clut!* went the lawn mower until, Noah heard a hissing noise.

"S-s-s-s-stop! Ple-e-e-a-s-s-s-s-e stop!" It was Mrs Green Grass Snake, who had made a nest in the long grass for her babies.

"Oh dear!" said Noah. He stopped mowing at once. "I'll go and trim my hedge instead.

So Noah got his shears and began clipping the hedge. *Snip, snip, snip, snip, snip!*

"Stop! Please stop!" twittered a voice anxiously. It was Mr Robin Redbreast. He had made a nest for his wife in the hedge, and their eggs were nearly ready to hatch.

"Oh dear!" said Noah. He stopped clipping the hedge at once. "I'll go and dig my vegetable patch instead."

Noah got his spade and began digging. *Scrunch-clump. Scrunch-clump-clump!*

"Ooo lovely!" said all the grubs and worms, squiggling around in the freshly dug earth.

"Well," said Noah, "I'm glad there's SOMETHING I can do in my garden today!"

30 The Little Monsters Race

The little monsters, Meeny, Miny and Mo were having a race. Everything is the wrong way round on Pongo, so they were starting at the Finish.

A Pongo pig waved his flag.

"Ready . . . steady . . . stop!" squeaked the Pongo pig. Pigs on Pongo don't snort – they squeak like mice.

Meeny, Miny and Mo ran off, once round a rugged rock and back again. Miny got to the Starting Post first, Meeny was next and last came Mo.

"Mo is the winner!" squeaked the Pongo pig.

Pongo *is* a very muddly place to live!

 31 Little Bear and the Sunflowers

Little Bear has been sowing some sunflower seeds in pots. The seeds have grown into little plants, and are ready to put in the garden.

Little Bear carries the plants to the flower bed.

"You'll need a trowel and a fork," says Mr Bear.

"And my watering can," says Little Bear. So they go to the shed and collect all the things he will need.

Little Bear digs a hole, just big enough for one sunflower plant. Mr Bear shows him how to tap the bottom of the pot with his trowel, to loosen the soil.

"Now the plant will come out easily," he says.

Little Bear gently lifts the plant out of the pot, and puts it into the hole. He spreads earth around the plant with his fork, and presses it down firmly with his paws.

"Well done," says Mr Bear.

Then Little Bear plants the other sunflowers in the same way.

"There's just one more important job to do," says Mr Bear. Little Bear thinks for a moment.

"I have to water them!" he says. So Mr Bear helps Little Bear fill his watering can, and Little Bear waters each plant carefully.

After that Little Bear watered his sunflowers every day and watched them grow. They grew and they grew and they grew until one day they burst into bright yellow sunflowers.

"They're the biggest flowers in the garden," says Little Bear proudly. "And I grew them all myself."

1 Hoot Learns to Fly

Doctor Dog and Nurse Kitty are visiting Mrs Owl today.

"It's young Hoot," screeches Mrs Owl from her nest, high in the pine tree. "He's afraid to fly."

Young Hoot is sitting nervously on a branch.

"It's such a long way down," he chirps.

Doctor Dog looks at Hoot.

"I'm not very good at climbing trees," he says.

"I'll go," says Nurse Kitty brightly.

Nurse Kitty scrambles up the trunk. She reaches for the first branch . . . and the next. A family of rabbits have gathered at the bottom of the tree to watch. It is exciting watching Nurse Kitty climb higher and higher.

Suddenly there is a *crack!* and a branch snaps under her paw.

"Help!" cries Nurse Kitty.

"Hold on," says Doctor Dog.

Nurse Kitty remembers there is a blanket in her First Aid box. "Quick! Spread the blanket out below," she shouts to Doctor Dog.

Doctor Dog and the rabbits each hold a corner of the blanket, so that Nurse Kitty can jump into it without hurting herself.

"One, two, three . . . jump!" shouts Doctor Dog.

Nurse Kitty falls into the blanket and bounces out safely.

Meanwhile Hoot has been watching from above. "That looks fun," he says. "I think I'll try it." And, before Doctor Dog can say anything, Hoot spreads his wings and plunges down to the blanket.

"Hoo, hoo, hoo!" cries Hoot. "I'm flying!"

"I'm glad you can fly," says Nurse Kitty.
"Now I won't have to climb that tree again!"

2 A Stitch in Time

Here's a needle, there's a thread,
Here is dolly's broken head.
Stitch it neatly,
Stitch it plain,
'til dolly looks herself again.

3 Clay Play

Roll it in a ball,
Stretch it if you can.
Squeeze it into arms and legs
To make a bendy man.

Roll it up again,
Now what will you make;
A pizza, car or aeroplane?

Oh no, a wriggly snake!

4 Tooth Fairies

Why do the fairies take our teeth?
It does seem very funny,
To take a tooth that's fallen out
And leave behind some money.

5 My New Puppy

Pickle's a bundle of trouble,
He got Gran's knitting in a muddle;
Chewed a slipper and, what's more
Made muddy paw marks on the floor.
So I said, "Pickle, behave! Come when I call."
Now, when he's alseep . . . he's no trouble at all.

123

6 Camping Out

It was a warm June evening. Ben and his friend, Joshua were going to sleep in a tent at the bottom of the garden. It was the first time the boys had camped out, and they were very excited.

Ben's mum helped them take things to the tent. They made several journeys with sleeping bags, pillows, pyjamas and slippers. Ben took a puzzle book, his best racing car, two teddies and a tin of toffees. Joshua had brought his cuddly lamb, an action robot and some chocolate.

"You'll need a torch," said Ben's dad.

"May we have some lemonade?" asked Ben.

"And crisps?" asked Joshua. "In case we get hungry."

When everything was in the tent, Ben's mum said, "Goodness! There's hardly any room for you boys."

"We'll leave a door open, just in case . . ." said Ben's dad.

Then they zipped up the tent and went back to the house.

Soon it was dark. The boys snuggled into their sleeping bags. They ate crisps and sweets by torchlight, and drank their lemonade. The campers giggled and talked in whispers until Ben thought he heard a noise. *Snuff, snuffle, snuff!*

"What was that?" whispered Joshua sitting up.

And whatever it was went, *snuff, snuffle, snap!*

Ben and Joshua listened in silence. The moon shone through the branches of a tree. It cast twiggy shadows over the tent, like bony fingers scratching to get in.

Then an owl swooped low screeching, *Whoooeep! Whoooeep!*

"I'm scared," said Ben, hugging his teddies.

"So am I," said Joshua, squeezing Lamb.

Slowly, the boys unzipped the tent and peered out. Ben's house seemed a long way away, but there were lights in the windows and the back door was open.

Ben and Joshua pulled on their slippers, crawled out of the tent and RAN up the dark and spooky garden, home.

"I thought you were camping," said Ben's dad.

"There were fierce animals outside our tent," explained Ben.

"And a witch was trying to get us," said Joshua.

"Oh, I see," said Ben's mum, as she followed the boys upstairs to bed. "Well, you had better camp IN tonight – you can camp OUT another time!"

7 Mouse Shoes

My birthday shoes are very nice,
But when I walk they squeak, like mice.
I wore them all around the house,
And Mum said, "Listen, where's that mouse?"

I tried to creep across the floor,
But they squeaked louder than before.
Then Puss pounced on my shoes in play,
And now the squeak has gone away.

8 The Queen of Hearts

You've heard about the Queen of Hearts
And how she made a plate of tarts?

That wasn't all the queen could cook,
She often took her cookery book
And opened it to find the page
Where stuffings were, of thyme and sage
With which to stuff a bird or two,
When she had nothing else to do.

Or, with a crown upon her head
The queen would bake a loaf of bread;
A treacle sponge, a chocolate cake.
But what a mess the queen did make.
She left the kitchen sink piled high
With dirty pots and pans - oh my!
And every sticky bowl and cup,
She NEVER did the washing up!

9 Big Things

Jumbo jets and
Fairground wheels,
A bright hot-air balloon;
Planet Earth,
The pyramids,
A rocket to the moon.

Elephants and
Ocean ships,
Rocky mountains high;
A city full of busy streets,
The dark and starry sky.

Dinosaurs and
Dumper trucks,
A giant forest tree;
The world around seems very BIG
To someone small like me.

10 Ten Little Monkeys

Ten little monkeys swinging on a line,
One let go . . . then there were nine.

Nine little monkeys climbing on a gate,
One slipped off . . . then there were eight.

Eight little monkeys flying up to heaven,
One flew away . . . then there were seven.

Seven little monkeys playing with some bricks,
One toppled over . . . then there were six.

Six little monkeys going for a drive,
One got left behind . . . then there were five.

Five little monkeys knocking at the door,
One ran inside . . . then there were four.

Four little monkeys sitting down to tea,
One felt sick . . . then there were three.

Three little monkeys make a sailing crew,
One fell overboard . . . then there were two.

Two little monkeys basking in the sun,
One got too hot . . . then there was one.

One little monkey standing all alone,
Went to find the other nine . . . then there were NONE.

11 Katie Runs Away

Katie kitten had a new brother, George. Ma and Pa Purrkins were very proud of George, even though he made a lot of extra work.

One evening Katie took her cuddly rabbit to Ma.

"Could you make Rabbit some new trousers please?" she asked.

"Not now," said Ma. "I'm bathing George."

Katie went to find Pa. "Will you read me a story?" she asked.

"Not now, Katie," said Pa. "I'm too tired. George kept waking up last night, and I've hardly slept a wink!"

Another day Katie said, "Can we go to the swings?"

"Not now," said Ma. "I'm feeding George."

Katie asked Pa, "Will *you* take me to the park?"

"Not now, Katie," said Pa. "I've got to make a playpen for George."

Ma and Pa were *always* busy with George these days. Katie felt left out and unwanted. She wasn't sure she liked having a new brother. And one afternoon Katie ran away.

She put Rabbit, a dress and her special blanket in a case, and crept out of the house. She went into the garden and hid in the shed. No one will find me here, thought Katie.

Meanwhile Ma and Pa had been searching for Katie all round the house. They looked upstairs and downstairs, but she was nowhere to be seen. Then they went outside.

"Katie! Katie! Where are you?" they called. Ma and Pa sounded very worried.

When Katie heard them calling, she began to cry. She held Rabbit tightly and sobbed into his long furry ears.

"Listen!" said Ma.

She opened the shed door, and found Katie in a dark corner.

Ma picked Katie up and gave her a big kiss. Pa was behind, carrying George.

"Kake-ee!" cried George holding out his paws.

"We all missed you," said Pa.

That evening Katie played with George and helped Ma put him to bed. Then Pa read Katie a story, while Ma made Rabbit a new pair of trousers.

"Tomorrow," said Pa when he had finished reading, "we'll all find time to go to the swings."

And they did. Ma and Pa Purrkins, Katie and George.

12 Team Games

Last week I joined the Blue team
And strange to tell, but true,
The other teams all won a race –
Every team but Blue.

Today I ran in the Red team,
And then Miss Ellis said,
"Well done Yellows, Greens and Blues!
Bad luck, those in Red."

So now I don't know what to do,
Which colour should I choose?
Whatever colour team I'M in . . .
That colour seems to lose!

13 A Thank You Letter

To the witch in Creepy Wood,
Your *Book of Spells* is really good.
I've tried the one on page sixteen,
It turned my sister Anne pale green.
At first I thought it was a joke
When Anne began to hop and croak.
But now she's sitting on a log -
A full-grown fat and ugly frog.

I wonder, could you please explain
How to change her back again?

Thank you for my birthday book.
Yours sincerely,

Raymond Cook.

P.S. *Please write soon - my sister looks very cross.*

14 Time

It's odd how time goes quickly,
When I'm busy having fun.
And Mum says, "Time to stop now."
When it seems I've just begun.

Or how it goes so slowly,
When I'm adding up my sums.
It takes me *hours* to count them
On my fingers, toes and thumbs.

But clocks and watches tell us
When to work and sleep and play.
So when I've learnt to tell the time,
I'll *know* the time of day.

15 The Selfish Dog

There was once a dog called Fletcher who lived on a farm. He had plenty to eat every day, and spent most of his time snoozing. One afternoon, having eaten a good lunch, Fletcher ambled across the farmyard. He wandered into the stable where the cart horses lived, but they were both out working in the fields.

Fletcher looked around for a comfortable bed. There was a pile of hay which looked soft and warm. Just the place! thought Fletcher. So he lay down in the hay and fell asleep.

At last the horses came home, tired and hungry after a hard day's work. As they hurried into the stable Fletcher woke up.

"Go away!" he snarled.

Fletcher bared his teeth and growled ferociously. You would have thought he was guarding a hoard of meaty bones.

"That's our hay!" said the horses. But they were too frightened to go near.

Just then Belinda, the farm cat, walked in. She lived in the stable, and the horses were her friends. Belinda sprang at Fletcher.

"Be off!" she hissed. "The horses are hungry for their supper."

Well, Fletcher took one look at Belinda's sharp claws and went. But as he trotted out of the stable he remarked,

"What a fuss about some dry old hay. I wouldn't eat that stuff, even if I were starving."

"Selfish dog," said Belinda scornfully.

"Yes," said the horses, munching happily. "Fletcher didn't want the hay himself, and he didn't want us to have it either!"

16 The Pot of Gold

Once upon a time there was a little old woman who lived by the sea. The little old woman was poor, and all she had to eat were the pumpkins she grew in her garden.

One day the little old woman looked out of her window and saw a rainbow. Now she knew that if she could reach the end of the rainbow, she would find a pot of gold.

"I'll go at once," said the little old woman to herself. But before she went, she made a pumpkin pie and put it in the oven for supper.

Then the little old woman set off. She walked this way, that way and round about the other way until, she came to the end of the rainbow. Sure enough, there was the pot of gold.

The little old woman was about to pick it up, when a dragon popped his head out of a cave.

The dragon, who was guarding the gold, looked surprised. He hadn't seen anyone for years.

"Stop!" he roared. But it sounded more like a cough, than a roar.

"Why?" asked the little old woman.

The dragon thought for a moment. "I can't remember," he said.

The little old woman felt sorry for the dragon.

"Why don't we share the gold?" she suggested.

132

"Hm, well," said the dragon thoughtfully.

"You could come and live with me by the sea," said the little old woman.

The dragon gazed up at the sky, as if to consider this offer carefully. He had always *wanted* to go to the seaside. "I might," he said.

"There's pumpkin pie for supper . . ." coaxed the little old woman.

"Done!" cried the dragon, who loved pumpkin pie more than anything in the whole world. And he roared a happy roar.

So the little old woman took the pot of gold, climbed on the dragon's back and they flew home. And from that day on, the little old woman and the dragon lived very happily together – and ate pumpkin pie every day.

17 Fancy Dress Party

I've been to a fancy dress party
Lots of my friends were there;
Stephanie went as a sunflower,
John was a grizzly bear.
William was great as a wizard,
Hannah looked just like a witch,
And Martin (who came as a monster)
Said his costume was making him itch.
David dressed up as a robot,
Nicolas came as a clown,
And I went as a butterfly . . .

But
my
wings
kept
falling
down!

133

18) A Picnic in Noah's Park

It was a hot June afternoon and Noah was getting ready to go for a picnic, by the river. He packed a basket with some sandwiches, cakes and lemonade, and was about to set off when Mrs Rabbit and her babies came along.

"I'm going for a picnic," said Noah.

"Can we come?" asked Mrs Rabbit.

"Of course," said Noah.

So Noah packed some carrots for the rabbits. The picnic basket was quite heavy.

Noah and the rabbits were about to set off when three bears came along.

"We're going for a picnic," said Noah.

"Can we come?" asked the bears.

Noah said they could, and he packed three large jars of honey for the bears. Now the picnic basket was very heavy.

Noah, the rabbits and the bears were about to set off when two monkeys came along.

"We're going for a picnic," said Noah.

"Can we come?" asked the monkeys.

Of course Noah said they could. Somehow he managed to find room in his picnic basket for two large bunches of bananas for the monkeys. But the basket was much too heavy to carry.

Noah, the rabbits, the bears and the monkeys were wondering what to do when an elephant came along.

"I'll carry your basket for you," said the elephant, "and you can ALL ride on my back to the river."

So Noah, the rabbits, the bears, and the monkeys had a wonderful picnic – and they all shared their food with the elephant!

19 Bedtime Bees

If counting sheep
To fall asleep
Makes *baas* inside your head;
Try counting bees
And, if you please,
Hear soft sweet *hums* instead.

20 Summertime

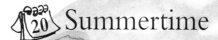

Summer's coming,
Bees humming,
Flowers growing,
Rivers flowing,
Sun stronger,
Days longer,
Crickets playing,
Corn swaying,
Raindrops falling,
Songbirds calling . . . summer's here!

21 A Sunny Spell

Did you know that on the first day of summer, fairies have a holiday? Well they do. The good fairy, Florence was going to the seaside. She packed her swimsuit, gave her wand a twirl and . . . *Ping!* off she went.

Florence landed on the beach with a bump. It was a hot sunny day, so she went for a swim in the sea. Florence was floating on her back when she saw a tiny black cloud. It was right over the place where she was swimming. Then she felt a drop of rain. And another. Hm! thought Florence. How odd.

It was the wicked witch Grizzle up to her no good tricks again. The fairies called her Grumpy Grizzle because she was always in a bad mood. And now Grizzle was trying to spoil Florence's holiday by making it rain.

Florence ran and got her wand. She gave it a couple of twirls and said some magic words;

Rain, rain go away,
I want a sunny holiday!

In a sprinkle of stardust, the raincloud vanished and there was a clear blue sky. "I hope my sunny spell will last," said Florence.

And I'm happy to tell you, it did.

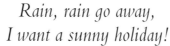

22 Honey Sandwiches

Mrs Bear is getting Little Bear's lunch-box ready to take to school. Little Bear helps to pack some of his favourite food; a strawberrry milk-shake, a bag of crisps and an apple.

"What sandwiches would you like today?" asks Mrs Bear.

"Honey, please," says Little Bear.

"You had honey sandwiches yesterday," says Mrs Bear. "And the day before. How about something else for a change?"

Little Bear can't think of anything else.

Mrs Bear looks in the cupboard.

"You could have; raspberry jam, lemon curd, crunchy peanut butter or chocolate spread," she suggests.

"Ummm . . . what else?" asks Little Bear.

"There's fish paste, cheese or mushy banana," says Mrs Bear.

Little Bear shakes his head. "What I'd like," he says. "What I'd really, *really* like is sandwiches with lots and lots of . . . HONEY!"

Mrs Bear laughs and cuts some slices of crusty bread. Then she spreads them with butter and thick, sticky honey.

"Yum-eeee!" says Little Bear, swinging his lunch-box all the way to school. "I've got my favourite lunch today!"

23 Silly See-Saw

The billy kids were playing in the park. They had a go on the swings, the slide and the roundabout. Then they saw something new. It was a see-saw.

"I wonder what it does?" said the billy kids.

One end of the see-saw was up in the air. The other end was down on the ground. The billy kids went to sit on it. But they both sat at the lower end.

"Silly see-saw," they said. "It doesn't do anything."

Just then the park keeper came along. "Silly billies!" laughed the park keeper. "You must sit one at *each* end. Then see what happens."

The park keeper helped one billy kid to sit at the other end of the see-saw. "Hold on tight," he said.

The see-saw went up and down, up and down.

"Wow!" said one billy kid, high in the air.

"Weee!" said the other, going down fast.

And they both agreed the see-saw wasn't so silly after all.

137

24 Dinosaur Hunt

Mrs MacGee was looking after the children one sunny afternoon. Lucy and Neil were hunting for a toy dinosaur Mrs MacGee had hidden in the garden.

"I wonder where it is?" said Lucy.

"That would be telling," said Mrs MacGee.

"Give us a clue," said Neil.

"I'll say 'warm' when you're near it, 'cold' when you're not," said Mrs MacGee.

Lucy looked near the gate.

"Cold," said Mrs MacGee.

"What about me?" asked Neil, peering under a bush.

"Freezing," said Mrs MacGee.

Lucy searched in the flower bed.

"Warmer," said Mrs MacGee.

Neil ran to the rockery and searched for the dinosaur there.

"Quite hot," said Mrs MacGee.

Then Lucy and Neil hunted among the rocks and flowers together.

"What are we now?" asked Neil.

"Very hot," said Mrs MacGee.

"It must be here *somewhere*," said Lucy, lifting a stone . . .

"Sizzling hot!" said Mrs MacGee.

"FOUND IT!" cried Lucy and Neil together.

"Just as well," said Mrs MacGee. "It's time for tea."

25 My Chair Bus

Climb aboard my chair bus
There's room for all you bears.
Piggie can be the conductor,
Collecting all the fares.

First stop, the library
Then off to the shops and school;
Down and round by the football ground
And on to the swimming pool.

Now my bus is full up
So home without delay.
Everyone back to the toy box,
No more rides today!

26 The Old Doll's House

One Saturday morning Jessica and her mum and dad went to a jumble sale. There were lots of people at the Town Hall jostling for bargains.

"Hold my hand," said Jessica's mum, as they pushed through the crowd.

They made their way to a stall piled high with things for the kitchen. "There are some useful things here," said Mum. They hadn't been there long when Jessica looked around.

"Where's Dad?" she asked.

"I expect he's found the junk stall," said Mum.

She asked her mum to take her there, but Mum was busy buying a jug. So Jessica slipped away and found Dad. He was carrying a large box.

"What's in there?" she asked.

"Aha," said Dad mysteriously.

When they got home, Dad took the big box to his shed in the garden. Jessica was curious to know what Dad had bought, so she crept to the door and peeped in. To her surprise there on the workbench was a DOLL'S HOUSE! Jessica gasped and her dad turned round.

"This was supposed to be a surprise," he said. "Come and see."

Jessica looked at the doll's house. Paint was peeling from the walls, some of the windows were broken and the furniture inside was covered in dust.

"I'll soon have this fixed up," said Dad. "You can help."

They spent all Saturday afternoon cleaning and mending the old doll's house. Dad gave it a coat of paint and put in new windows.

Jessica dusted the little tables and chairs, and washed all the tiny cups and plates. Mum gave her some scraps of material for curtains, and helped to hang them at the windows.

Soon the doll's house looked as good as new. Dad carried it up to Jessica's room, and she played with the house until bedtime. When her mum and dad came to say goodnight Jessica said,

"I'm glad we went to the jumble sale."

"Dad usually finds some old junk to bring home," said Mum.

"Not today," said Dad. "The doll's house looked very shabby, but I knew it could be repaired."

"Thank you," said Jessica. "It's the best doll's house in the world."

27 A Shopping List

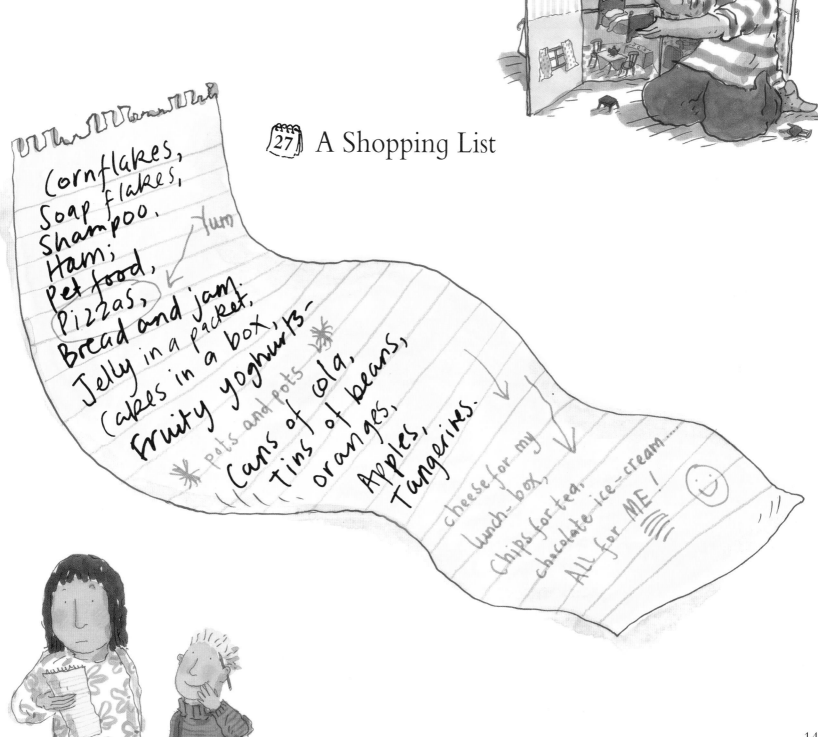

Cornflakes,
Soap flakes,
Shampoo,
Ham,
Pet food,
Pizzas,   Yum
Bread and jam,
Jelly in a packet,
Cakes in a box,
Fruity yoghurts,
Pots and pots
Cans of cola,
tins of beans,
oranges,
Apples,
Tangerines.
cheese for my lunch-box,
Chips for tea,
chocolate ice-cream...
ALL for ME!

28 Four Seasons Farm

It was summertime and Robert was staying on his uncle's farm. One afternoon Robert and Uncle Jack went for a walk. They went through a gate which had *Four Seasons Farm* on it.

"What are seasons?" asked Robert.

"They're the four different times of the year," said his uncle.

"What are they called?" said Robert.

"Spring, summer, autumn and winter," said his uncle. "One season follows another, every year."

As they walked, Uncle Jack talked about the seasons.

"In springtime the crops begin to grow," he said. "You can see tiny leaf buds on the trees and hedges. Everything starts to wake up at the beginning of the year."

Along the way they saw sheep grazing by the river.

"Have you got any lambs?" asked Robert.

"The lambs were born in spring, " said Uncle Jack. "It's summertime now. They're growing up."

"What happens in summer?" asked Robert.

"Let's look around," said his uncle.

Robert pointed to the trees and hedges.

"They're covered with leaves," he said.

"That's right," said Uncle Jack.

"There are lots of flowers too in summer, and the sun helps to ripen the crops."

They walked through a field of corn, which was turning yellow.

"This crop will soon be ready to harvest," said Uncle Jack.

"What comes next?" asked Robert. "I've forgotten."

"Autumn," said his uncle. "That's the season when some leaves change colour. They turn orange, yellow and brown. And you'll find nuts and berries along the hedgerow in the autumn."

"Then the squirrels can collect them and store them, can't they?" said Robert.

"Yes," said his uncle. "It's a busy time of year. The apples in the orchard are ready to pick then. We pack them in boxes and take them to market."

"I know what comes next," said Robert. "Winter!"

"The coldest season of the year," said Uncle Jack. "When it snows, we bring the cows into the barn for shelter."

"I like snow," said Robert.

"I expect you do!" said his uncle. "But it's the time of year when nature has a rest. The trees are bare, and some animals curl up and sleep all through winter."

"Then the seasons start all over again," said Robert.

"That's right," said his uncle. "We plough the fields in the autumn and winter months, ready to sow more crops in the spring."

"So that's why this is called Four Seasons Farm!" said Robert.

And they walked back to the farmhouse.

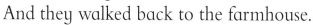

143

29 A Tall Story

This is a story about a man called Mr Short who was very tall. Mr Short had legs as long as telegraph poles, and his head was always in the clouds. It wasn't easy being as tall as Mr Short. He was lonely because he had nobody his own size to talk to. And, to make matters worse, children made fun of his name.

"*Silly old Shorty long legs!*" they sang.

One windy afternoon Mr Short went for a walk. The wind blew the clouds about like anything that day. Suddenly, something flew right past his nose. It was a kite. The kite tossed and tugged at its string until it got away and tangled itself on a tower.

Mr Short looked down. Way below him the children were pointing to the kite and crying because they couldn't get it down. Mr Short was so tall, the top of the tower only came up to his chin.

"I'll help you," he said.

So Mr Short took two steps on his legs as long as telegraph poles, and unhooked the kite – easy as winking. The children were very happy. They thanked Mr Short for helping them, and were never unkind to him again.

Then last week Mr Short got a job. The perfect job for a tall man like Mr Short. Can you guess what it is? He got a job as a window cleaner. The only window cleaner in the world who doesn't need a ladder! He made lots of friends and was never lonely again. Which is a nice way to end a tall story, isn't it?

30 How High is the Sky?

How high is the sky?
Does it stop at the top of the ozone layer,
Somewhere up there, in the stratosphere?
If not,
Then what?

1 The Pig Family Go Camping

Mr and Mrs Pig and the piglets are having a camping holiday. They have found a nice spot by the river to put up their tent. Potter and the piglets are excited. They have never been camping before.

"Pass me the hammer, please Potter," says Mr Pig. "I'll have this tent up in no time."

Mr Pig hits the tent peg hard. BANG.

"*Ouch! Ooo! Ouch!*" wails Mr Pig. He has hit his trotter instead.

"There, there," says Mrs Pig, bandaging his sore foot.

At last the tent is ready. It is only just big enough for Mr and Mrs Pig and the piglets to fit inside.

"Move over, Potter," say the other two piglets.

Potter rolls to one side and the tent falls down.

"Oh, no!" says Mrs Pig.

Later that evening when Mr Pig has put the tent up *again*, the Pig family wriggle into their sleeping bags and go to sleep. They are all snoring soundly when . . . it starts to rain. *Drip. Drip. Drip.* Big drops of water splash on to Mr Pig's nose.

"I've just remembered something," says Mr Pig.

"What?" says Mrs Pig, waking up.

"I forgot to fix the hole in the tent," he says.

"Good job I brought my umbrella," says Mrs Pig. And she opens her umbrella to keep them all dry.

Next day the sun is shining. While Mr Pig mends the hole, Mrs Pig and the piglets cook breakfast over a camp fire. Then they all go for a walk by the river. Potter and the piglets look for tadpoles and dabble their trotters in the water.

"I like camping," says Potter. "It's fun."

Mr and Mrs Pig smile. "Yes," they say, "it IS!"

The Runaway Teaset  2

The teapot and the teacups
Were climbing off the tray.
With the milk jug and the sugar bowl,
They planned to run away.

"No more work for us!" they cried,
And jumped down to the floor . . .
But as they crashed,
Each one was smashed.
The teaset was no more.

3 Shells

A shrimp has a shell,
A crab does as well
And so does a tortoise and snail;
But the best shells for me
Are the ones by the sea.
I'm collecting them up in my pail.

4 The Big Parade

Today is the day of the Big Parade. Police Constable Fox is busy leading the procession down the High Street. "This way," he says marching proudly at the head of the parade. He is followed by;
a troupe of drum majorettes in their smart uniforms, the Fire Brigade in a shiny, new fire engine,
a lorry full of dainty dancers in costumes, the Rag Tag Tiger Band playing jazz,
a cranky car full of clowns squirting water, a bus load of monkeys waving flags,
a dumper truck full of balloons and the Town Band marching on behind . . .
Tan tara. Tan tara. Boom! Boom! Boom!

147

5 Flying

I went in an aeroplane,
It was exciting as can be.
We flew to a country far away,
To a hotel by the sea.

We checked in at the airport,
And then we had to wait
A long time to board the plane,
Through the Departure Gate.

The aircraft was on the tarmac,
An enormous silver bird.
The engines were screaming so loudly,
I couldn't hear a word.

A hostess was on board to greet us,
She showed us to our seats.
I sat by a window with Teddy
And ate some chewy sweets.

Then we taxied down the runway -
I hugged Teddy tight.
The engines ROARED, the aircraft soared,
We took off on my very first flight.

We flew over the rooftops,
Above the hills and trees;
Way up high, in a clear blue sky,
Across the salty seas.

6 Doctor Dog on Holiday

Doctor Dog arrives at the surgery one morning looking very tired.

"You need a holiday," says Nurse Kitty.

Doctor Dog thinks Nurse Kitty is right. He packs his bags for a holiday in the mountains straightaway.

"Long walks and lots of fresh air will do me good," he says.

Nurse Kitty waves him goodbye. "I'll look after all your patients while you're away," she says.

Doctor Dog drives his car to the mountains. Then he parks and goes for a walk. He hasn't gone far when he hears a terrible moaning noise. It is coming from the forest.

"Ow, ooo, ow!" A grizzly bear has been stung on the nose by a bee. It is very painful.

Doctor Dog stops to help. "It's a good job I brought my First Aid kit," he says and puts some ointment on the bear's sore nose.

"Thank you," says the bear. "My nose feels much better."

Doctor Dog walks on and in a little while he meets a wolf. The wolf is howling at the top of his voice.

"Yowoool!" he howls. "I've got toothache."

"Oh dear!" says Doctor Dog. "Let me see what I can do."

Doctor Dog pulls the tooth out and the wolf grins happily.

"Thank you," he says. "I feel much better."

At the top of the mountain, Doctor Dog sits down to rest. Suddenly an eagle swoops down, screeching loudly.

"Caw, caw, caw!" cries the eagle. "I've hurt my leg."

Doctor Dog examines the leg carefully and bandages it up.

"Thank you," says the eagle. "My leg feels better already."

When Doctor Dog's busy holiday is over, he goes back to the surgery.

He finds Nurse Kitty relaxing in a chair.

"Did you have many patients?" asks Doctor Dog.

"No," says Nurse Kitty. "I think they all went on holiday."

"Yes," says Doctor Dog. "They were all in the mountains with me!"

Dooley's Night Out

Dooley sat on the garden wall feeling miserable. Laura, the little girl he belonged to, had gone to bed and forgotten to bring him in. The evening shadows grew longer until the sun slipped down over the rooftops and it was dark.

The house where Dooley lived was at the end of a street. In the daytime it was full of people, busy shopping. Now the street was empty and strangely quiet. As the moon shone down, Dooley looked at the big front door of the house. He hoped it would open, and Laura would come running out to rescue him. But the door stayed firmly shut and, one by one, the lights in the house went out.

Dooley was alone and afraid.

He listened as a clock in the town struck midnight. Twelve slow chimes then . . . footsteps. Someone was walking slowly and steadily along the street, stopping now and then. It was a policeman on patrol checking that all the shops were safely locked for the night. When the policeman got to Dooley's house he stopped.

"You're out late," he said, giving Dooley a pat on the head.

Dooley cheered up a bit after that. It was comforting to know that someone was about. Dooley gazed up at the stars and tried to count them. He had counted up to twenty when a bell rang out shrilly from somewhere down the street. It was a fire alarm!

A few minutes later a fire engine came racing along. Oily, black smoke was pouring out of an office window. Suddenly the quiet street was full of fire officers putting out the fire.

Dooley could see everything. It was very exciting. By three o'clock the fire was out and the fire engine went away.

In the silence that followed Dooley was beginning to feel lonely again when *CRASH!* A dustbin and all its rubbish clattered to the ground. A cat had been scavenging for food and had found some tasty bones to eat. Dooley hoped the cat would stay and talk to him, but she was in a hurry.

"I'm off!" said the cat, jumping over the wall.

After that Dooley didn't have a moment to himself. At dawn the birds woke up and started singing. At six o'clock factory workers came walking down the street, on their way to work. And at seven o'clock the postman delivered letters to Laura's house.

"You're up early," the postman told Dooley cheerfully.

Then at eight o'clock the best thing happened. The big front door opened and Laura came running into the garden. She took Dooley off the wall and hugged him tight. "Oh Dooley!" she whispered, "I forgot all about you. You must have been so lonely."

Dooley smiled to himself. I would have been, he thought, but there was so much going on last night!

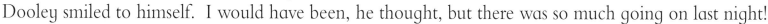

8 Whales

Whales have tails as big as sails
And little eyes that blink,
And holes to blow the water out –
Otherwise they'd sink.

A Tale of a Tail

Oliver Puppy looked at himself in the mirror one morning. He liked his ears. He thought his nose was wonderful. But when he turned to look at his tail . . . Oliver Puppy sighed. It was short and thin. Hardly a tail at all. "It will grow," said his mum. "You'll see."

Oliver went to see his friends on the farm. First he visited a cow. She had a long swishy tail. "I wish I had a tail like yours," said Oliver. The cow mooed with laughter. "My tail is much too long for a puppy," she said.

Next Oliver went to see a horse. He was flicking flies away with his long thick tail. "I wish I had a tail like yours," said Oliver. The horse neighed with laughter. "My tail is much too big for a puppy," he said.

So Oliver went to see the chickens. A cockerel was strutting around the yard. He had a magnificent feathery tail. "I wish I had a tail like yours," said Oliver. The cockerel crowed with laughter. "Just think what you'd look like with feathers!" he said.

Oliver felt sad. All his friends had beautiful tails. If only his would grow. Oliver Puppy went home to his mum. She wagged her long hairy tail and licked him all over.

"I wish I had a tail like yours," said Oliver.

His mum smiled. "You will," she said. "Wait and see."

From that day on Oliver Puppy grew bigger and bigger until, one day he looked in the mirror again. He liked his ears. His nose was better than ever and, when he turned to look at his tail . . . there was the best tail he had ever seen.

"I told you it would grow," said his mum. "It's a fine tail."

"And just right for ME!" said Oliver proudly.

 **Sweet Surprise**

Something smells good in the kitchen,
Sugary, spicy and sweet.
A pudding? A pie? What can it be?
Mum's making a special treat.

So I peep into the kitchen
And as you all can see,
That sugary, spicy, sweet surprise
Is a BIRTHDAY CAKE for me!

To a Snail

Snail, snail move faster,
Your slowness will end in disaster.
Mrs Blackbird's on your trail . . .
Please go faster, little snail.

Under My Bed

Something lives under my bed
It was there again last night,
Grunting and growling like anything -
It gave me an awful fright.

Does it have hairy legs,
With feet and terrible claws?
Will it start to chew me up
In its slobbering toothy jaws?

This morning I felt brave
So Elephant, Tiger and me
All looked carefully under the bed
To see what it could be . . .

But there was nothing there.

153

13 Pairs

A pair of gloves,
A pair of socks,
A pair of shoes in a cardboard box.
Two arm chairs,
Two little mice,
Two green pears,
Twice as nice.
Twins in a pram,
Birds in a tree,
A pair of rascals - you and me!

14 Things I Can Do

I can . . .
Stand on my head,
Touch my toes,
Do up my buttons and
Tie my bows.
Help with the shopping,
Feed the birds,
Choose my own books and
Read little words.
Splash in my bath,
Climb the stairs,
Kneel at my bedside and
Say my prayers.

15 My Roof Garden

I have a garden way up high
Where sunflowers almost reach the sky.
Sweet peas and forget-me-nots
Grow round about the chimney pots,
And pansies smile and nod their heads
Along my roof-top flower beds.
No prettier flowers have I found
In any garden on the ground.

17 A Good Rainy Day

A world without water –
What do you think?
No water to cook with,
Wash in or drink.

No puddles to splash in,
No rivers or seas;
No pools to go swimming
Whenever you please.

No rain for the garden,
For forests and crops.
All creatures need water –
Without it, life stops.

So next time it rains
And its too wet to play,
Just say to yourself,
It's a good rainy day!

16 Sports Day

I went in for the sack race,
I was doing all right until
Josh bumped into Lizzie
And I fell over Bill.

We *almost* came first in the three-legged race,
Me and Daisy Peep.
Then our legs got muddled up somehow,
And we landed in a heap.

But my best race was running,
Bang! went the starting gun.
I ran like the wind to the finishing line
And everyone cheered, "You've WON!"

18 The Missing Scissors

It was the last day of term at Katie kitten's school. Mrs Tabby, the teacher had asked everyone to tidy the classroom. Katie and her friend Tim were Mrs Tabby's special helpers that day.

"Can you find all the scissors for me?" said Mrs Tabby. "There should be ten pairs in the scissor box."

Katie and Tim looked in the box but there were only **three** pairs of scissors in it.

Katie did a sum on her paws. "We've got to find **seven** pairs of scissors," she said.

They began hunting round the classroom. First Tim found one pair of scissors under a chair and another pair on top of the bookshelf. He put them in the box with the others. Now there were five pairs of scissors in the box. "There are still five missing," said Tim.

Katie looked around. She saw one pair at the bottom of the cupboard and another pair in front of the nature table. She put them in the box and counted up.

"How are you getting on?" said Mrs Tabby.

"There are seven pairs in here," said Katie. "We've got to find another three."

After that Tim found one pair of scissors behind the dressing-up box and another in the sand tray. "Nine pairs in the box," said Tim.

"Just one more pair to find," said Katie.

They hunted high and low for the scissors but they couldn't see them anywhere. Katie and Tim looked disappointed. They went to Mrs Tabby to tell her that the tenth pair was missing. Mrs Tabby was busy at her desk and when Katie peeped over the top, THERE were the missing scissors, under a ball of string.

"Naughty me!" said Mrs Tabby. "I took the scissors out of the box and forgot to put them back."

So Katie put the last pair of missing scissors in the box.

"Well done!" said Mrs Tabby.

At going home time, Mrs Tabby gave everyone a sweet from a big tin. But she gave an extra one to Katie and Tim for finding all those scissors.

19 Odd Socks

Two, four, six, eight
Socks go on the line.
So why when they come off again,
is the odd one always mine?

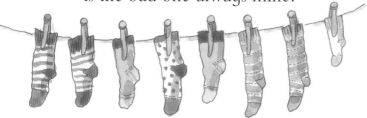

20 A Monstrous Recipe

Buckets of beetles,
Tubs of toads,
Smelly fishheads - loads and loads.
Lumpy gravy,
Mouldy stew,
Stir it up with a worm or two.
Put in a pot.
Cook for a week...

Now you know what monsters eat!

21 My New Bike

I got a new bike for my birthday -
The best one in the shop.
It's got gears to make it go faster
And brakes so I can stop.
There's a bell to ring on the handlebars –
So everyone, clear the way!
I'm racing off on my bicycle
Around the park today.

22 Sid Squid

Down at the bottom of the deep blue sea
There lived a squid called Sid.
He ate up little fishes,
That's what that squid Sid did.

157

23 Sophie and the Tooth Fairies

One evening, just before bedtime, Sophie lost a tooth. She had been wiggling her loose tooth all day and, quite suddenly, it had come out.

"Pop it under your pillow for the fairies," said Sophie's mum.

"Why do they want my tooth?" asked Sophie.

"I'm not sure," said Mum, "but they'll leave you some money."

Sophie put her tooth under the pillow and settled down. Sophie felt sleepy but she wanted to see the fairies. As she lay there listening for fairy footsteps . . . a voice whispered from her pillow,

"Left, right, hold on tight.
We're off to the Land of Dreams tonight."

It was Sophie's magic bed, taking her off on another adventure. It sprang up on its legs and was out of the bedroom in a blink. Sophie sat up and saw that her covers had turned into huge butterfly wings. They flapped gently up and down, through a rainbow.

"We're nearly there," said the bed.

"Where?" asked Sophie.

"Fairyland, of course," it said.

They glided silently into a woodland glade full of flowers. To her surprise, Sophie found she was no bigger than a rosebud. She and the bed had shrunk! Suddenly they were surrounded by fairy folk, all chattering at once.

"Have you brought a tooth?" asked one fairy called Amber.

Sophie showed the fairy her tooth.

"It's lovely!" she said. "Follow me."

Sophie jumped off the bed and found that she could fly. Her tiny wings fluttered faster and faster, as she followed Amber to a toadstool. "This is where we make our jewellery," she explained.

Inside there were rows of workbenches. Elves sat sorting and polishing teeth, while fairies threaded them to make tiny necklaces.

"Those are for the fairy babies," said Amber.

Then she took Sophie to meet an old fairy. "This is Jade," said Amber. "She is the Royal Necklace Maker."

"I use only the finest, pearliest teeth to make jewellery for the Fairy Queen," said Jade. She showed Sophie a necklace she was making.

"I need just one more tooth to finish this for the queen. It must be ready in time for the Summer Ball tonight."

"Will mine do?" asked Sophie. She gave Jade her tooth.

"Perfect!" exclaimed the old fairy. "Look, it fits right here in the middle. The most important tooth of all."

When the Royal Necklace Maker had finished the necklace, Sophie took it to the queen. She curtsied and wobbled a bit.

"Welcome to Fairyland," said the queen. "And thank you for bringing your tooth. You must come to the Summer Ball."

Sophie looked down at her pyjamas.

"I haven't anything to wear," she said.

The Fairy Queen waved her wand and Sophie gasped as her pyjamas turned into a ball gown. It glittered with stardust. So Sophie went to the Summer Ball and danced with all the fairy folk. But as they whirled around Sophie heard a voice whispering,

> *"Left, right, hold on tight.*
> *Home again before morning light."*

and in no time, Sophie's magic bed whisked her back to the bedroom.

Next morning Mum said, "Have the fairies been?"

Sophie looked under her pillow. Her tooth had gone and in its place was a silver coin.

"Fancy that," said Mum. "I wonder what those fairies wanted your tooth for?"

"They put it in a necklace for the Fairy Queen," said Sophie.

"Of course," said Mum. "Why didn't I think of that. Now hop out of bed or you'll be late for school."

When Sophie looked down at her pyjamas, she saw something her mum hadn't noticed. Her pyjamas were sparkling with stardust!

24 The Garden Seaside

The school holidays had just begun. One afternoon Toby and Sarah were playing in the garden. Mum and Dad were at work, so Grandad was looking after the children. It was hot and sunny. The flats and houses all around seemed to make the day feel even hotter.

"I wish we were at the seaside today," said Toby.

"You're going in two weeks," said Grandad. "When Mum and Dad begin their holidays."

"Two weeks!" sighed Sarah. "I can't wait that long."

Grandad knew how they felt. "Perhaps we could make a seaside in the garden," he said. "Let's see what we can find."

First Grandad looked in the garage. He found Toby and Sarah's old paddling pool, folded up at the back. The children helped to carry it into the garden and Grandad said, "Now for the hose!"

Toby held the hose while Sarah turned on the tap. *Whoosh!* Water squirted into the pool and soon it was full.

"Time for a swim," said Grandad.

The children raced indoors, changed into their swimming things and *SPLASH! SPLOSH!* - jumped into the paddling pool. They were splashing about when Mrs Dickens, who lived next door, leaned over the fence.

"We're swimming in the sea," said Toby.

"Are you now?" said Mrs Dickens. "Well, I've got some rocks and sand left over from my new rockery, and an old washing-up bowl. You could make a rock pool."

"Thank you!" said Sarah.

So Grandad took a wheelbarrow and fetched the rocks, sand and bowl from Mrs Dickens. Then Toby and Sarah had fun making the pool. They put little stones in the water and Toby fetched his sailing-boat from the bathroom. While they were playing, Mrs Dickens leaned over the fence again. She was holding three big ice creams.

"You can't have a seaside without ices," she said, handing one each to Grandad and the children.

Later that afternoon Mum and Dad came home from work. They found Sarah and Toby 'fishing' in the rock pool. Grandad was dozing in a garden chair.

"We're at the seaside," said Toby.

"So I see," said Dad.

"Well," said Mum, "we'd better have fish and chips for tea."

"Can Mrs Dickens come too?" asked Sarah.

"Of course," said Mum. "We'll all have tea at the seaside!"

25 Ghost Train

We went for a ride on the ghost train,
Dominic, Gemma and me.
We screamed going into a tunnel,
It was scary as can be.

A skeleton glowed in the darkness,
Spiders dangled from threads,
The train rattled into a churchyard
And ghosts flew over our heads.

The haunted house was spooky –
A vampire grinned with glee.
It opened its fangs to take a bite . . .
From Dominic, Gemma and me.

Then we raced into the sunshine,
We all looked ghostly white.
And we said, "That was FANTASTIC –
We've all had a wonderful fright!"

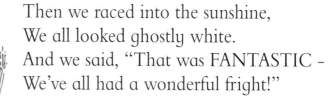

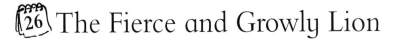

The Fierce and Growly Lion

One day Giraffe With a Scarf was nibbling leaves from the top of the Tum Tum tree when a lion cub came by. *Grrrrr!* growled Little Cub as fiercely as he could.

"Hello," said Giraffe With a Scarf. "Who are you?"

"I'm a fierce and growly lion," said Little Cub. "All animals are afraid of me."

"Well, I'm not," said Giraffe With a Scarf. And he went on eating his leaves.

Little Cub looked disappointed, so he trotted off to find someone else to scare. He met Mr Bear looking for honey. *Grrrrr!* growled Little Cub.

"How do you do," said Mr Bear politely. "I don't think we've met before."

"I'm a fierce and growly lion," said Little Cub. "All animals are afraid of me."

"Afraid of you?" said Mr Bear. "Not me!" And he went on searching for honey.

There must be *somebody* who's afraid of me, thought Little Cub. He gave a loud roar. *GRRRRR!* And just then Humpy Camel walked by. "Who's that purring?" he said.

"I'm not purring, I'm ROARING," said Little Cub. "I'm a fierce and growly lion. All animals are afraid of me."

"Well, I'm not," said Humpy Camel. "But I think I know an animal who might be. Follow me."

So Little Cub followed Humpy Camel to a pool in the forest.

"Have a look in there," said Humpy Camel with a smile.

Little Cub peered into the dark pool and growled his loudest, fiercest growl. *GRRRRRRRRRR!* And to his surprise, there in the pool was an animal growling back at him. *GRRRRRRRRRR!*

"Oh help!" said Little Cub, seeing his reflection in the pool.

Humpy Camel laughed. "The only animal who is afraid of you Little Cub, is . . . yourself!"

27 Polly the Pony

Polly the pony was sad. Polly's owner, Vicky, had grown too big for her. For weeks Vicky had been riding a new horse called Midnight, while Polly stayed behind in the field.

"It's not fair," Polly told her friend Patch, the sheepdog, one day.

"At least you don't have to look after silly sheep, like I do," said Patch. "Things will get better, you'll see."

And to Polly's surprise they did. A little girl called Charlotte came to stay on the farm where Polly lived. Charlotte loved ponies and she made friends with Polly straightaway.

"You can ride Polly as often as you like," said Vicky.

"Thank you!" said Charlotte.

Charlotte spent hours with Polly. She groomed her coat 'til it shone, and brushed her mane and tail. On fine days Charlotte and Vicky went riding together; Polly and Midnight trotting one behind the other, Polly holding her head high and swishing her tail. Sometimes they went galloping across the fields, jumping fences and splashing through puddles. On those days Polly and Midnight would come home tired, muddy and ready for their feed.

One evening while Polly was dozing in the stable, Patch came to see her. "Happy?" he asked.

"Yes," said Polly thoughtfully, "but I'm sad about one thing."

"What now?" said Patch.

"When the holidays are over . . . Charlotte will be going away."

"Not far away," said Patch. "I've heard Charlotte is coming to live near the farm."

It was true. Charlotte's parents had bought a new house just down the lane. So Charlotte saw Polly every day, and went riding with Vicky whenever she could. "You're the best pony in the world," Charlotte often whispered to 'her' pony. It made Polly feel special.

So the next time Patch saw Polly he said, "*Now* are you happy?"

And Polly said, "Yes, yes, yes, I am."

163

28 The Wise and Foolish Man

Once upon a time there was a wise man who spent much of his time gazing at the stars. He was fascinated by those tiny dots of twinkling lights, so far away in the heavens. He thought he could learn a lot from them.

One evening as he was walking along, his head tilted back to look into the starry sky, he fell into a deep hole.

"Help! Help!" cried the wise man. "Someone please get me out."

But his cries drifted into the night. There was no one around to hear him - only the stars, way up high.

In the morning a peasant woman came along, collecting wood for her fire. She heard the man's cries coming from the hole.

"Well," said the woman helping him out of trouble, "what a foolish fellow you are. You were so busy looking up at the sky, you forgot to look under your feet!"

And the man had to agree she was right!

29 Little Bear's Day in Bed

Little Bear is not very well today. Mrs Bear takes his temperature.

"You are hotter than usual," she says. "You must stay in bed until you're better."

Later Little Bear's friends call round to play.

"I can't come out," says Little Bear. "I don't feel well."

Little Bear's friends are sorry for him. "Get well soon," they say. "We'll come again tomorrow."

At lunchtime Mr Bear brings Little Bear some food on a tray.

"I don't feel like eating," says Little Bear.

"Dear me," says Mr Bear. "You are a poorly bear. Would you like me to read you a story?"

But Little Bear shakes his head. He doesn't feel like his favourite storybook either.

"Well, go to sleep, Little Bear," says Mr Bear gently. "I expect you'll feel better when you wake up."

Little Bear sleeps all afternoon and when he wakes, his tummy is rumbling. Hm! thinks Little Bear, it must be teatime. Mrs Bear comes to see how he is. She finds Little Bear sitting up and playing with his toys.

"How about some milk and a honey sandwich?" she says.

"Yes, please," says Little Bear. "I'm hungry!"

After tea Mr Bear walks into the bedroom. He is hiding something behind his back. "How's the patient?" he asks.

"Much better," says Little Bear jumping out of bed.

"What have you got in your paws?"

"Guess which paw it's in to find out," teases Mr Bear.

"Left or right?"

Little Bear thinks hard. "L-e-f -f...no, RIGHT!"

"Right first time!" says Mr Bear holding up a chocolate bar. "But are you well enough to eat it?"

"Yes," says Little Bear, "I am!"

"A day in bed did you good," says Mrs Bear with a smile. "Tomorrow you can go out to play."

Noah and the Big Fish

One breezy day Noah decided to go sailing on the lake. Flip and Flap, the penguins, wanted to go too.

"All right," said Noah, "you can be my crew."

Noah's sailing boat was moored by a jetty. He held the boat steady while the penguins jumped aboard. Then Noah climbed in and hoisted the sail, while Flip and Flap pulled up the anchor. The wind filled the sail and soon the boat was skimming across the lake.

"This is fun," said Flip and Flap as the waves sprayed them with foam. But when they got to the middle of the lake, the wind stopped blowing. The sail flapped against the mast, and the boat drifted to a stop.

"Oh dear!" said Noah. "What now?"

Flip and Flap knew what to do. While Noah sat in the boat waiting for a breeze, they went swimming. The penguins had a lovely time diving off the deck and splashing into the lake.

Meanwhile Noah waited and waited. But there wasn't a puff of wind anywhere. Suddenly Flip and Flap gave a shout. A great big fish swam by and popped his head up to say hello.

"Please help us," said Noah.

The big fish was very friendly and said he would rescue them.

"Just tie a rope to my tail," he said.

So Noah tied a rope to the fish's tail and *Swish! Swish!* they were off. The fish towed the sailing boat safely back to shore.

"Thank you very much," said Noah and the penguins.

The big fish said goodbye and, with a mighty swish of his tail, he was gone.

Just then a puff of wind blew across the lake and whisked Noah's hat off.

"What a silly sailing day!" said Noah.

31 Magic Bubbles

The little monsters Meeny, Miny and Mo were having a birthday party. Planet Pongo birthdays don't happen just once a year - little monsters have birthdays whenever they feel like them.

A wizard arrived at the party in a puff of smoke.

"Wizard Fizz at your service," said the wizard.

"Birthday Party entertainment a speciality." And he gave Meeny, Miny and Mo some magic bubble mix.

"Thank you," said the little monsters excitedly.

Meeny, Miny and Mo blew three big bubbles and waited to see what would happen. Suddenly, they found themselves floating high above the ground. The little monsters were *inside* the bubbles!

"Look at me!" cried Meeny, turning a somersault.

Miny and Mo's bubbles bumped into a mountain and bounced off again like giant rubber balls.

The magic bubbles floated up and up, 'til they touched the stars. Then they went round the moon and down again, and landed on Pongo with a *Poof! Bang! Pop!*

"That was fun," said Meeny, Miny and Mo as they picked themselves up off the ground. They looked around for Wizard Fizz, but he had vanished into thin air. Wizards are like that on Pongo. There one minute, gone the next - just like those magic bubbles.

Poof! Bang! Pop!

1 Where is Everybody?

Where is Clare?
At the fair,
In a rocket ship.

Where is Wayne?
In a train,
On a seaside trip.

Where is James?
Playing games,
Hiding in a tree.

Where is Jason?
At the basin,
Making cakes for tea.

Where is Mary?
With her canary,
Teaching it to sing.

Where is Mark?
In the park,
Swinging on a swing.

Where is Lisa?
Eating pizza
With her best friend Paul.

Where is Kerry?
On a ferry.
Did you find them all?

2 Air

Air, air,
Everywhere.
I can't see it,
I can't hold it,
But I know it's there.

3 Squiggle and Squirms

Squiggle and Squirms,
Two little worms
Lived happily in a ditch.
But I'm sorry to say,
Neither worm to this day
Could ever tell which end was which.

4 Ripe Red Cherries

Ripe red cherries on the tree
When I grow up, what will I be?

One for a spaceman,
Two for a witch,
Three for a princess, fair and rich.
Four for a pirate,
Five for a clown,
Six for a king with a golden crown.

5 Some Treasure!

Sam and Wallace were chugging along in *The Topsy Turvy* when they caught sight of the pirate ship, *The Bag o' Bones*, anchored near a beach.

"I wonder what Captain Scuttlebutt and those Saucy Pirates are up to?" said Sam.

"Looks like they're fishing," said Wallace.

Sam steered his boat towards them to take a closer look. Snitch and Snatch were up on deck with fishing rods, while Captain Scuttlebutt was busy reading a map.

"Hm!" said Sam. "You don't need a map to catch fish. I wouldn't be surprised if they weren't fishing for - *treasure*."

It was true. There *was* a sunken treasure chest to be found there somewhere, and Captain Scuttlebutt was trying to find it. Suddenly Snitch gave a shout.

"I've caught something!" he yelled excitedly.

Snatch helped to pull it in.

"Heave ho, me hearties," said Captain Scuttlebutt. "We've found the treasure."

But oh dear! All Snitch had caught was a rusty pram.

"Some treasure!" laughed Sam.

Captain Scuttlebutt was furious.

"Keep fishing," he ordered.

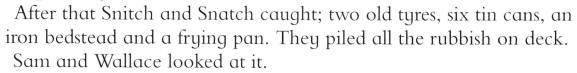

After that Snitch and Snatch caught; two old tyres, six tin cans, an iron bedstead and a frying pan. They piled all the rubbish on deck. Sam and Wallace looked at it.

"The things people throw in the sea!" said Sam. "Let's take them all to the rubbish dump where they belong."

So Sam helped the pirates take all the rubbish to a dump. The coastguard saw them, and was very pleased.

"We didn't find any treasure," said Captain Scuttlebutt crossly.

"No," said the coastguard, "but you fished a lot of old rubbish out of the sea. You can look for treasure another day!"

6 All in a Day

What can you do in a day?
Wake in the morning,
Wash and dress.
Eat your breakfast - make a mess.
Paint your face,
Dance and sing,
Fish in the pond with a stick and string.
Feed the ducks,
Go for a walk,
Draw a picture with a piece of chalk.
Scrub your hands,
Have some tea,
Watch a programme on T.V.
Read a book,
Hop into bed . . .
Dream all night, you sleepyhead!

7 Playtime

Puss says,
"Mouse, mouse, come out of your house,
We could have some fun.

I'll chase you round about the chairs,
Down the hall and up the stairs

To see how fast you run.
Mouse, mouse what do you say -
Will you come and play today?"

And mouse says,

"No!"

8 Cuckoo! Cuckoo!

Hickory, dickory, dock,
The mouse ran up the clock.
Cuckoo! Cuckoo!
The clock struck two -
And gave the mouse a shock.

9 The Lost Blanket

One hot sunny day, the Purrkins family were getting ready to go to the beach. Ma packed a big picnic basket with lots of food; fishpaste sandwiches, biscuits, cream cakes and plenty of milk. Pa packed a beach bag with towels, paddling shoes and sun hats.

"Don't forget the fishing nets," said Ma. "We might catch some shrimps."

Katie kitten was busy packing too. She put her bucket and spade, cuddly rabbit and beach ball in a basket. Her baby brother, George, was 'helping' by taking things out.

"Go and find your blanket," said Katie, putting everything back.

A little later Pa Purrkins put the picnic basket, the beach bag, fishing nets and Katie's basket in the car.

"Are we ready?" he said.

"I think so," said Ma. "Come along George."

"I can't find my blankings," said George.

"Oh, no!" sighed Katie.

So Ma, Pa and Katie went to look for George's blanket. It was blue and a bit grubby, but it was George's favourite thing. He NEVER went anywhere without it. The Purrkins spent a long time hunting all over the house; upstairs, downstairs, in drawers, under chairs . . . but George's blanket was nowhere to be seen.

"I want my blankings!" cried George.

At last Katie said, "I think I know where it *might* be." She had remembered seeing it somewhere while she was packing her things. . .

They all went out to the car again and looked in Katie's basket - and THERE was George's blanket, right at the bottom.

"My blankings!" said George.

"He must have put it there without me seeing it," said Katie.

"But you found it," said Ma. "Well done."

"And *now*," said Pa, "let's go to the beach, and catch some shrimps for tea!"

10 Spotted Shingly Shangly Beasts

Spotted Shingly Shangly Beasts
Are seaweed green and scaly.
They gobble up enormous feasts
Of cod and herring daily.

They like to sleep in rocky caves
(I've often heard them snore);
Or dip their toes and tails in waves
That splash upon the shore.

And sometimes when the moon is bright
I have seen them prancing –
Across the sands, all through the night,
These curious beasts go dancing.

11 Pets at the Vet

Pets at the vet
Waiting,
With bandaged paws
Bumps and sores.
Ears sagging
Tails not wagging.
Three dogs and a cat,
A long-tailed rat,
All need attention,
Not to mention
A very sick snake –
Thin as a rake
Or the fish in a jar
And a budgerigar.

Waiting . . .

"Next, please," says the vet
Smiling,
And takes good care
Of each patient there.
With medicine and pills
He cures the ills
Of the dogs and the cat
And the long-tailed rat,
The very sick snake –
Thin as a rake,
And the fish in a jar
And the budgerigar.
Until,

There are no more pets
At the vet.

12 The Heat Wave

Mr and Mrs Goat and their billy kids were spending a holiday at the seaside. One sunny day Mr Goat was reading his newspaper on the beach. He was looking at the weather forecast.

"Phew!" said Mr Goat. "We're going to have a heat wave today."

The billy kids had never seen a *heat* wave before, so they ran down to the water's edge to wait for it to come. They waited and waited. The waves splashed over their feet.

"Ooo!" shouted the first billy kid, "the water is *cold.*"

"I wonder if the heat wave will be very hot," said the other.

After they had been there for a little while, Mr Goat came to see what they were doing.

"We're waiting for the heat wave," they told him.

Mr Goat laughed.

"Silly billies," he said. "You won't find a heat wave in the sea. It's a name for hot weather. I can feel the sun getting hotter already."

Suddenly there was a loud *SPLASH!* as Mrs Goat jumped into the water. "Come for a swim," she said, "it's lovely and cool. Just the place to be on a hot summer's day!"

13 Granny's Teddy Bear

Granny says,
"My teddy bear is very old –
About a hundred years
And parts of him are bare and worn
Around his paws and ears.
His tummy once was round and fat,
Stuffed full of yellow straw;
It hasn't got much left of that –
He's thinner than before."

When she was young and Ted was new
They'd play for hours, you see.
Now *we* have fun together,
Gran's teddy bear and me.

14 I Saw a Dinosaur

I saw a dinosaur
Down by the seashore
Eating ice-creams
One, two, three, four.

15 My Sand Castle

I've made a castle out of sand
With towers and turrets – very grand,
And all around, a proper moat
Where I can float my sailing boat.

But when the tide has turned once more
And splashy waves roll to the shore,
I know the sea will wash away
The castle that I made today.

16 The Little Bridge

There was once a little bridge that crossed a river. Every day drivers drove their cars and vans over him from one side of town to the other. ***Honk, honk, clatter, clatter.***

As time went by more and more traffic used the little bridge. Heavy trucks and coaches full of holidaymakers visited the town.

Brrm, brrm, rumble, rumble.

Sometimes the little bridge sighed under all that weight and one day he began to crumble. A sign was put up saying, 'BRIDGE CLOSED' and all the drivers had to go a long way round to cross the river. There were traffic jams everywhere.

The days that followed were strangely quiet. A bridge builder came to examine the little bridge. He wrote notes in his notebook and went away. The little bridge began to worry about what would happen next. Then, early one morning, workmen came with a bulldozer and crane to build a NEW bridge nearby.

For weeks the little bridge watched the new bridge being built. It was made of concrete and steel, strong enough to carry the heaviest loads. When it was finished, the little bridge was sure he would be forgotten. No one will want me now, he thought sadly.

But he was mistaken. A few days before the new bridge was opened, workmen came to repair him. They replaced his crumbling stones with good ones, and gave his lamps and railings a coat of glossy paint.

"Just in time for the Grand Opening," said one workman. "That new bridge is fine for traffic . . . but there's nowhere for PEOPLE to walk!"

It was true. From that day on the little bridge was as busy as ever, with townsfolk walking to and fro.

Pitter, patter, chitter, chatter, *hop,* *skip,* ***jump!***

📅17 The Dreamboat

Patrick loved to travel at bedtime. He could go round the world and back again.

On **Monday** Patrick sat in his dreamboat. "Let's go somewhere hot tonight," he said. So they did. Patrick sailed to a tropical island in his dreamboat. It was full of parrots and palm trees. While they were there Patrick picked a bunch of bananas.

On **Tuesday** Patrick sat in his dreamboat. "Let's go somewhere cold tonight," he said. So first they went to the South Pole and met some penguins, playing on the ice. Then they sailed to the North Pole. "I'm freezing," said Patrick, snuggling up to a polar bear.

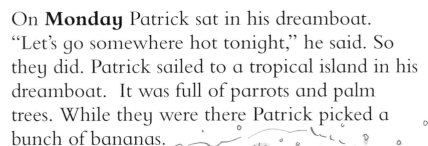

On **Wednesday** Patrick sat in his dreamboat. "Let's go swimming tonight," he said. The dreamboat took Patrick to the ocean. There were cat fish and dog fish swimming below the waves. Patrick dived in and . . . bumped into a swordfish. "Ouch!" he cried. And woke up.

On **Thursday** Patrick sat in his dreamboat. "Let's go to a desert," he said. And off they went. They found a pyramid and Patrick went inside. He saw some mummies standing in a row. "Where are the daddies?" asked Patrick. But there was no reply.

On **Friday** Patrick sat in his dreamboat. "Let's go to a jungle," he said. There were tigers and snakes in the jungle. Patrick swung through the trees. "I'm Tarzan," he cried. "Look at me!"

On **Saturday** Patrick sat in his dreamboat. "Let's climb a mountain tonight," he said. There were eagles and wolves on the mountain, and Patrick could see the whole world from the top.

On **Sunday** Patrick sat in his dreamboat. He couldn't think where to go next. He had been round the world and back again. Patrick yawned and snuggled under the blankets. "Tonight," he said, "I'll just stay home in BED!"

18 Rainbows

When it's muddly sort of weather
With rain and sun together,
You may look, and way up high
See a rainbow in the sky.
And before it fades away
Name each colour – can you say?

Red orange yellow green blue indigo violet

177

19 Tickets, Please!

Mr and Mrs Bear and Little Bear are going out for the day.
They are visiting the city. First they go to the station.
Mr Bear buys three yellow tickets for the train journey.

"Can I hold the tickets?" asks Little Bear.

"Here you are," says Mr Bear. "Don't drop them."

On the train a ticket inspector calls out, "Tickets, please!"
Little Bear hands the tickets to him.

"Thank you," he says, checking the tickets and handing
them back to Little Bear. "You can put these in your back pack."

When they arrive, the bears go sightseeing on a special bus.

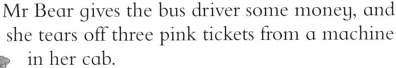

"All aboard!" says the bus driver.

"Fares, please."

Mr Bear gives the bus driver some money, and
she tears off three pink tickets from a machine
in her cab.

"Can I hold them?" asks Little Bear.

"Here you are," says the bus driver.

The bears go round the city on the
bus, past all the big shops, hotels and
museums. At last they stop outside the
gates to a park. Little Bear hears some
music playing. Fairground music.

"Ooo!" says Little Bear. "Can we go to the fair?"

"Of course," says Mrs Bear.

There is a kiosk inside the park with a man selling tickets for the rides. "Roll up! Roll up!" he shouts. "Get your tickets here."

This time Mrs Bear buys the tickets and gives them to Little Bear.

"More tickets," she says. "These ones are green."

Little Bear puts them in his back pack with the others. Then the bears spend all afternoon at the fair.

At home that evening, before Little Bear gets ready for bed, he looks in his back pack. It is full of tickets! He has yellow train tickets, pink bus tickets and green tickets for the fairground.

"I think I'll be a ticket inspector, when I grow up," says Little Bear sleepily. "Tickets, please!"

20 Out in the Garden

Out in the garden, early in the morning
See the little lettuces growing in a row.
Then along come some rabbits,
With nibbly little habits . . .
Now there are NO more lettuces growing in a row.

21) Sneezy Weeds

The day Zoe found some strange-looking flowers growing at the bottom of the garden, things were never quite the same. She picked a few and showed them to her dad.

"Weeds," said Dad, "they're no good."

Zoe knew differently. "They're *magic*," she said mysteriously, sniffing them. "*AH-TISHOO!* "

"So much for your magic flowers," said Dad. "They just make you sneeze. Sneezy Weeds, that's what I call them."

"But when you sneeze, you make a wish," persisted Zoe. "*That's* when the magic begins!"

Zoe took the Sneezy Weeds behind the garden shed. She wanted to wish on her own.

"I wish, I wish, I wish . . . I could have my very own pony," Zoe whispered, her eyes shut tight. When she opened them, she saw a pony standing in the garden, munching the hedge.

"It worked!" cried Zoe, hugging the pony happily. And she rode him over the fields and far away.

On a rainy afternoon, Zoe sniffed a Sneezy Weed, sneezed once and wished for an elephant. Sure enough, one arrived immediately. The elephant lifted her with his trunk, and they marched off to Africa. She was a bit late back for tea that day.

"Where have you been?" asked her dad.

"Africa," said Zoe.

"Really?" said Dad.

"Have we got any buns for the elephant?"

"What elephant?" said Dad.

"The one outside the window," said Zoe.

"Oh, *that* elephant," he said. "I'll see what I can find."

That night Zoe looked out of her bedroom window. She gazed up at the bright, silver moon and thought about the Sneezy Weeds.

"Tomorrow," she said, "I might go to the moon . . ."

And, believe it or not, she did.

22 A Whale of a Tale

Kelly's friend, Joe, was a deep-sea fisherman. He could tell wonderful stories.

"Did I tell you about the time I was swallowed by a whale?" said Joe.

Kelly's eyes opened wide. She shook her head.

"It was last August," began Joe. "I was fishing in the middle of the ocean when suddenly a giant wave tossed me out of my boat."

"What did you do?" said Kelly.

"I looked around for something to hold on to," said Joe. "Then, quite by chance, a whale swam by - the biggest whale you ever saw."

"Ooo," said Kelly.

"He opened his enormous mouth, and I found myself being swept along inside - like a spider swirling down a drain," said Joe.

"Were you scared?" asked Kelly.

"Not a bit," said Joe. "I went head-over-heals down his throat, bumped my head on his tonsils, and landed in his stomach. It was smelly down there, I can tell you. Talk about rotting fish!"

"What then?" said Kelly, hardly able to believe her ears.

"I met three sailors," said Joe. "They had been swallowed too."

"Three sailors!" said Kelly.

"Three or four," said Joe. "I can't remember exactly. But we all sang sea songs to pass the time. We were inside the whale for weeks. He swam right across the ocean, to the bottom of the world."

"How did you get out?" asked Kelly.

"The whale spat us out on an iceberg," said Joe. "He was a friendly whale, you see. It was his way of rescuing us. After that we sailed home on a passing ship."

"What a story!" said Kelly.

"I'm glad you liked it," said Joe. "There are plenty more where that came from!"

23 Much More Luke

Luke and Stephen were best friends, but Luke often boasted that he had more or bigger things than Stephen. For instance, when Stephen's cat had five kittens, Luke said,

"That's nothing. Our cat had *eight* kittens last week."

Then there was the time Stephen went fishing with his dad. Stephen caught a fish, and took it home for supper.

"It was this big," he told Luke. Stephen held his hands apart to show how big the fish had been.

"Well, when I went fishing with *my* dad," said Luke, "I caught a fish THIS big." He flung his arms as wide as he could. "It took two of us to carry it!"

One morning the two boys were having a race on their bicycles. Suddenly Stephen's wheel hit a stone. Stephen wobbled and collided with Luke, and they both fell off with a *bump!*

"Ow! My arm," cried Stephen.

"Bet my arm's worse," sniffed Luke.

Stephen's mum came out to see what was the matter.

"That's a nasty cut," she told Stephen. "We'd better get you to hospital."

"What about me?" asked Luke.

"Your arm looks sore," said Mum, "but I think it's just a scratch."

So Mum drove Stephen to the hospital, and Luke went too. A doctor in the Casualty Department examined Stephen's arm.

"You'll need some stitches," she said.

Luke showed the doctor his arm.

"Will I need stitches?" he asked.

"I don't think so," she said gently. "We'll find you a nice big plaster, instead."

Later, Stephen proudly showed Luke his arm.

"I've got SIX stitches," he boasted.

And for once – just for once – Luke said,

"That's MUCH MORE than me! "

24 August

August in,
Children play
On a seaside holiday.

Tide out,
Boats away
Sailing far beyond the bay.

Harvest in,
On the farm
All the hay is in the barn.

Sun out,
Weather fine,
Pack some food, it's picnic time!

25 Too Hot

It's too hot to growl,
Too hot to purr,
Too hot to run, wriggle or stir.

But,
It's just right for sighing,
Dreaming and lying
Down by the pool

Where it's cool . . . cool . . . cool.

26 The Man from Mars

As I was walking down the road
I met a man from Mars,
And when I asked him where he lived
He pointed to the stars.

"Go right around the Moon," he said,
"And straight on past the Sun,
Then left along the Milky Way -
That's where I come from."

But when I turned to look again,
The man from Mars had gone.

27 A Secret Place

I know a secret hiding place
Down by the apple tree,
And if you promise not to tell
I'll take you there with me.

It has a log where we can sit -
A mossy table too,
And a leafy sort of window
Where the sun comes shining through.

No one in the whole wide world
Could ever find us there;
So now you know about it -
It's a secret we can share.

183

Harry's Holiday Diary

Monday
My friend Leanne lost her rabbit called Hopper. We looked all round the garden and in the flower bed. Then Leanne's Dad shouted and we found Hopper eating a lettuce in the vegetable patch.

Tuesday
Daniel and Ashley came to play. We sat in our tree house and made up a password. *Twizzlegumdrum*. It's TOP SECRET and no one can come into our tree house without saying it. My big sister tried, but she doesn't know the right word.

Wednesday
We went swimming today. The water chute was brilliant. My sister screamed all the way down, but I didn't. Someone switched the machine on and we dived into the waves. They were really big.

Thursday
It rained all day. I made my bed into a star ship and flew to a strange planet. I saw some weird aliens. They tried to catch me, but I took off in my star ship at FULL SPEED.

Friday
Went to tea with Leanne. We had fish fingers, jelly and strawberry ice cream – my favourite. I told Leanne about the TOP SECRET password. Now she can come to the tree house too.

Saturday
I helped Dad wash the car. I squirted some water over my sister – *by mistake*. She thought I meant to do it and pulled my hair.

Sunday
We went to see Granny and Grandad on the farm. My sister and I helped to feed the pigs. One pig had seven piglets. One piglet fell into the trough and we had to lift him out. I am going to be a farmer when I grow up because I like pigs.

Harry's Diary

TOP Secret

29 I Can't Sleep!

Doctor Dog has been busy in the surgery all day.

"I'll go to bed early tonight," he says, "and have a good sleep."

Doctor Dog puts on his pyjamas, cleans his teeth and gets into bed.

He is soon fast alseep and snoring. Suddenly the telephone rings.

Drrring, drrring! Doctor Dog wakes with a jump and answers it.

It's young Mole. "I can't sleep," she says.

"It's night time," says Doctor Dog. "Moles are supposed to be awake. Go and dig a tunnel."

Then Doctor Dog puts the phone down and goes back to bed. He is dreaming peacefully when, the phone rings again. *Drrring, drrring!*

Doctor Dog answers it sleepily.

This time it's Mrs Owl's son, Hoot.

"I can't sleep," says Hoot.

"Owls are supposed to be awake at night," says Doctor Dog. "Go and fly round the woods."

Doctor Dog yawns and stumps back to bed. He closes his eyes and is just nodding off when *Drrring, drrring!* the telephone rings *again,* and Doctor Dog has to answer it. It's fox cub Freddy.

"I can't sleep," he says.

"Foxes are supposed to be awake at night," says Doctor Dog. "Go for a walk. You might see Mole and Hoot. They're awake too."

Next morning Doctor Dog is sound asleep. At seven o'clock his alarm clock goes *Cock-a-doodle-doo!* But Doctor Dog doesn't hear it. A little later the telephone rings. *Drrring, drrring! Drrring, drrring! Drrring, drrring!* It's Nurse Kitty, ringing from the surgery. When Doctor Dog answers it, all he can think to say is,

"I CAN'T SLEEP!"

"Well," says Nurse Kitty, "it's nine o'clock in the morning and there are lots of patients waiting here. You should be WIDE AWAKE!"

30 New Homes

One night there was a terrible storm in Noah's park. Thunder rumbled overhead, and a strong wind blew an oak tree down.

Early next morning some rooks came and perched on Noah's roof.

"Can we stay with you?" they asked. "The wind has blown our nests away."

"Yes," said Noah. "You can stay until you have built new ones."

Later, when Noah went into his garden, he found Mr and Mrs Squirrel on the lawn. They looked upset.

"Can we stay with you?" asked the squirrels. "The wind has blown our tree down."

"Of course," said Noah. "You can stay until you find somewhere else to live."

After that two owls, a family of mice and a toad came to see Noah. They had all lost their homes in the oak.

"I think," said Noah, "we had better go and look for another tree, where you can make new homes. My house is getting full up!"

So the rooks, the squirrels, the two owls, the family of mice and the toad all followed Noah into the forest. The storm had done a lot of damage; there were broken branches everywhere.

At last Noah spotted a huge oak, where all the animals could live. The rooks built their nests right at the top; the owls found a hollow in the trunk; the squirrels climbed about looking for acorns, while the mice and the toad burrowed around the roots.

"Now you've all got new homes, I can go back to mine," said Noah. "But please come and visit me soon."

"Thank you, Noah," said the animals. "We will!"

📅31 Molly, the Kitten

Miss Penny was an author. She had written lots of books for children but today, Miss Penny was having trouble writing one word. It was all because of Molly the kitten. Miss Penny had bought Molly from the pet shop a few days ago and, since the new kitten arrived, she had hardly any time for writing stories.

First, Molly needed feeding every four hours. "She will need a little to eat and drink often," the man in the pet shop advised. After meals Molly used her litter tray, so Miss Penny had to keep that clean and fresh. Then there was playtime. Miss Penny would roll a ping-pong ball along the floor, and watch Molly chase after it. Or, Molly would pounce on a piece of paper, pretending to catch a mouse. When Molly tired of play, she wanted cuddles and sleep. Miss Penny spent a lot of time with the kitten curled up on her lap.

But today Miss Penny was trying to write a story. 'Once upon a time . . .' she typed on her computer. Then Molly pounced on her foot.

"Ouch!" cried Miss Penny. The kitten had sharp claws.

Miss Penny tried again. 'Once upon a time there was . . .'

Molly jumped on the desk. *Pitter-pitter-pat* went her paws on the pencils until they rolled off the desk, one by one. *Clatter-clatter-clatter!* Miss Penny stopped and picked them up.

"Molly, I'm trying to work," she said. "Now, where was I?"

Miss Penny stared at her computer screen, to see what she had written. 'Once upon a time there was . . .' she read. "There was – what?" said Miss Penny.

For once she couldn't think what to say next. She looked up at the ceiling. She looked down on the floor. Then she looked at Molly.

"I know . . ." she said.

Which is how Miss Penny, the author, came to write a rather special story. Can you guess what it was called? That's right. *Molly, the Kitten*. And you've just read it!

 1 The Right Breakfast

Mrs Bird and her babies lived in the Tum Tum tree. Early one morning while Mrs Bird was out looking for food, Little Bird hopped out of the nest. "*Cheep, cheep, cheep!*" he cried.

Humpy Camel came to see what the noise was about.

"I'm hungry," said Little Bird. "I want something to eat."

"Try some of my hay," said Humpy Camel.

But Little Bird didn't like the taste of hay. Tears were beginning to roll down his beak, when Hee Haw Donkey walked by.

"I'm hungry!" said Little Bird.

"Try some of these," said Hee Haw Donkey, and showed Little Bird his patch of prickly thistles. Little Bird didn't like the taste of those either.

Then Mr Bear came along.

"I'm hungry!" said Little Bird.

"Try some of my honey," said Mr Bear. But Little Bird didn't like the taste of honey. He sat at the foot of the Tum Tum tree and sobbed. "*Cheep, cheep, cheep!*"

Giraffe With a Scarf was eating leaves and heard Little Bird. Just then Mrs Bird flew back to the nest, with food for all her babies.

"I'm sure your mum knows what you like to eat," said Giraffe With a Scarf. "Hop on my nose. I'll put you back in your nest."

"There you are Little Bird!" said Mrs Bird. And she popped a big, fat WORM into his beak.

"Ooo, lovely!" chirped Little Bird. "*That's* just what I like."

 ## 2 A Long Walk

Our teacher, Mrs York,
She took us for a walk,
We marched all day
Around the bay . . .

And didn't get home 'til dark.

3 Runaway Beans

The beans that I'm sowing
Keep growing and growing and growing and
growing and growing;
And if they don't stop
When they get to the top
I'll never know where they are going.

 ## 4 Fair Share

There are some selfish girls and boys
Who never want to share their toys,
Or offer round a sweet or two
Which kinder children often do.

I knew a meany little tot
Who sat alone and ate a lot
Of sticky, creamy chocolate cake
(The one he'd watched his mother bake.)

He never thought to leave a slice
For family, friends, the kitchen mice . . .
But ate up every single crumb,
As greedily he filled his tum
Until he looked quite pale and sick
And rang the doctor, "Please come quick!"
The doctor came and shook his head
And sent the greedy child to bed.
"Next time," he said, "there's cake for tea,
Just eat YOUR SHARE, and don't call me!"

5 Magic Paints

It was Katie Kitten's first day back at school after the summer holidays. Ma Purrkins kissed her goodbye.

"Work hard," she said.

That morning Katie was very busy. Mrs Tabby gave everyone in the class new books to do their sums in. Katie finished hers quickly and got them all right. So Mrs Tabby put a big smily face at the bottom of the page. Then Katie wrote her holiday diary, and read three pages from her reading book before dinnertime.

In the afternoon Mrs Tabby told everyone to put on their aprons; it was time for painting. Katie sat at a table next to her friend, Tim. They shared pots of YELLOW, RED and BLUE paints, and a jar of water to wash their brushes clean.

"I'm going to do paw prints," said Tim. He dipped his paw into the red paint, and covered his paper with splodges.

"I'm going to do a proper picture," said Katie.

She painted a house with a red roof and a blue door. Then she put a bright yellow sun in the sky. But when Katie went to paint some grass she said,

"Please, Mrs Tabby, I need GREEN paint."

"Just mix a little yellow and blue paint together," said Mrs Tabby, "and see what happens."

Katie mixed the two colours and, as if by magic, they made green! After that, Mrs Tabby showed her how to mix yellow and red to make ORANGE. So Katie finished her picture with lots of green grass and orange flowers in the garden.

At going home time she showed her picture to Ma.

"Ooo! that's lovely," said Ma.

"Mrs Tabby showed me how to make magic paints," said Katie.

"Did she?" said Ma. "It's amazing what you learn at school!"

6 Counting Letters

A B C D E F G,
How many insects can you see?

H I J K L M N,
How many women? How many men?

O P Q R S T U,
How many sailors in the crew?

V W X Y, last comes **Z,**
How many cats on the old tin shed?

7 On the Move

Traffic on the motorway,
Jets in the air,
Liners on the ocean waves
Sailing somewhere.

Trains on the railway track,
Vans on the road,
A motor-car transporter -
With a double load.

Buses in the High Street,
Barges on the river,
Motor-cycle messengers
With parcels to deliver.

Police cars in a hurry,
Tankers going slow
All of them are on the move,
Now think of some YOU know!

8 A Quiet Corner

There's a quiet corner in our classroom
Where I can curl up like a kitten on the cushions
To listen to a story
Or take a book from the shelf
And read one for myself,
Quietly.

9 Flying Cakes

It was Alfred Jones' birthday. His mum was upset. She had burnt his birthday cake, and there wasn't time to bake another one. So Alfred went to see his friend, Hilda Brimstone, who also lived in Moonshine Mansions. Hilda was a witch.

"Do you think you could magic a birthday cake?" asked Alfred.

"I should think so," said Hilda.

"No magic, please!" said Hilda's cat, Hubble.

Hilda took no notice. She thumbed through her spell book.

"Now let me see . . . *How to make; crocodiles, caterpillars - cakes*! What colour would you like?"

"Green, please," said Alfred.

Hilda muttered some magic words, clicked her fingers and . . . *bang!* A small green *snake* appeared, with a candle on its head.

"Nearly right," said Alfred.

"I knew it would go wrong," groaned Hubble.

Hilda looked confused and tried again. This time there was a puff of smoke and the room was filled with - fairy cakes. Alfred was a bit disappointed. They weren't quite what he had been expecting.

"Those fairy cakes have got real wings," said Hubble, "and they're flying away."

It was true. The fairy cakes were flying through an open door. Soon they were fluttering all over Moonshine Mansions. Alfred chased after them but he couldn't catch them.

Meanwhile Hilda was busy with another spell. Just as Alfred's friends were arriving for the party, there was a blinding flash - and the biggest green birthday cake landed on the tea table.

"Wow!" said Alfred. He thought Hilda was the cleverest witch ever.

At that moment Alfred's mum came into the room.

"How did that cake get here?" she said.

"It appeared by . . . magic," said Alfred truthfully.

"Did it now," said Mrs Jones. "Well, magic or not, it's the best cake I've ever seen. Happy Birthday Alfred!"

10 Sneezing

Sneeze on **Monday**, meet a witch,

Sneeze on **Tuesday**, fall in a ditch.

Sneeze on **Wednesday**, fly to the moon,

Sneeze on **Thursday**, whistle a tune.

Sneeze on **Friday**, make a wish,

Sneeze on **Saturday**, dance with a fish.

But sneeze on **Sunday**, that's really clever . . .

Good Luck will stay with you for EVER and EVER!

11 Imogen Claire

Imogen Claire
hasn't a care,
she will not brush or
comb her hair,
or wash her face,
or blow her nose.
But we suppose
that as she grows
she will
get
better.

12 Some Do's and Don'ts

I DON'T like cabbage
Or peas in my stew
I DON'T like beetroot, but
I DO love you.

I DON'T like the dark
Or spiders in my shoe
I DON'T like cobwebs, but
I DO love you.

I DON'T like shopping
Or waiting for the loo
I DON'T like crowds, but
I **DO** love you!

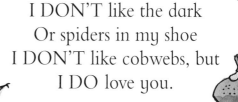
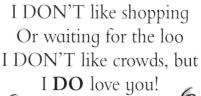
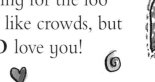

13 Fergus the Tractor's Busy Day

Malcolm was in the farmyard bright and early.

"We're going to be busy today," he told Fergus the tractor.

First Malcolm hitched a trailer to the tractor. Then he climbed into the cab and started the engine. Fergus had a powerful engine and great big wheels. They drove to the orchard, and found the fruit pickers already hard at work, picking apples and packing them in boxes.

"Let's load up," said Malcolm.

He steered Fergus slowly between neat rows of apple trees, stopping every now and then to load boxes on to the trailer. When it was full, they set off for market, down the lane, past the school and into town.

By late afternoon the load had been safely delivered. As Fergus hurried back to the farm, the empty trailer rattled along behind. They were just passing the school again, when Malcolm saw something blocking the road. The school bus had broken down.

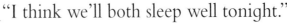

"We must help," said Malcolm.

The bus driver and the children were pleased to see them.

"Hop up on the trailer," said Malcolm. "We'll take you home."

Fergus waited while everyone clambered on board. Then he pulled the trailer round the village, stopping to let the children off near their homes.

"Goodbye and thank you for the ride!" they shouted.

It was dark by the time Malcolm and Fergus got back to the farm.

"What a busy day!" said Malcolm, giving Fergus a pat on the bonnet. "I think we'll both sleep well tonight."

14 The Little Fish

There was once a little fish who lived in a big river, that swished and swirled its way to the sea. All day the little fish swam and fed along the rocky river bed. He played chase with his brothers, and 'leap-fishy-leap' over the waterfall. At night he slept, tired and content, in a clump of reeds.

The little fish would have gone on living happily in this way but, he met a mischievous rat, swimming near the riverbank. The rat dared the little fish to be more adventurous.

"Swim to the sea," he said. "Life is much more exciting there."

The little fish decided to go at once, even though his brothers tried to stop him.

"The sea is a dangerous place," they warned.

But the little fish wouldn't listen. He flipped his tail and was off, skimming through the water. He swam all day and all night. The river got wider and wider until the little fish found himself in the sea. The water tasted very salty. Soon huge waves swept him far away from the river.

What an adventure! thought the little fish, feeling a tiny bit afraid.

Way out where the sea was deep, the little fish saw lots of other fish. There were small, stripy ones swimming in shoals, and strange round fish which looked like balloons. Suddenly, an enormous shark swam by with snapping jaws. The little fish darted off as fast as he could.

He was swimming so quickly, he didn't see the net. A gigantic fishing net was spread out under the waves, scooping up hundreds of silver, flapping fishes. The little fish swam right into it, and was hauled into a boat.

"Oh . . . what . . . an adventure!" cried the little fish, gasping for air.

Then a fisherman noticed him and laughed.

"You're much too little to eat," he said. And he threw the little fish back into the sea. *SPLASH!*

After that the little fish swam back to the river as fast as he could.

"No more adventures for me," he said.

195

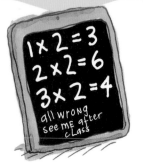

 The Toad Princess

Once upon a time there was a king and queen who had a son called Wilfred the Wonderful. To be honest Prince Wilfred wasn't all that wonderful; he had knobbly knees, his ears stuck out and he couldn't do his sums.

One day the king said, "It's time you got married, Wilfred. The world is full of beautiful princesses. You're sure to find a wife."

So Prince Wilfred got on his bicycle, and went all over the place searching for a bride. He met lots of princesses who were all very beautiful but they weren't too keen on him. "You've got knobbly knees," said one. "Your ears stick out," said another. "And you CAN'T DO SUMS," said a third.

Prince Wilfred pedalled home feeling sad. He had just opened the palace door when a toad hopped on his foot. It was fat with blobby brown warts.

"Yuk!" cried the prince.

The toad leapt on his shoulder, and whispered in his ear.

"Remember, remember,
I'm Princess September.
"One kiss and you'll see
The real, lovely me!"

"Kiss you!" shrieked Prince Wilfred. "Not likely."

"There's no need to be rude," said the toad, who really *was* a princess. "A wicked witch cast a spell on me - just because I tripped over her broomstick. Now I have to find a prince to kiss me and break the spell."

"Well, don't look at me," said Prince Wilfred.

"I AM looking at you," said the toad princess, smiling as sweetly as she could (for a toad that is). "I hear you haven't had much luck in finding a wife with your knobbly knees and sticky-out ears . . . and I could help you with your sums."

"Really?" said Prince Wilfred, suddenly looking at the toad princess with interest. "Can you do sums?"

"Add up, take away, *and* multiplication," she said.

That did it. Prince Wilfred thought she was the cleverest thing in the world. So he shut his eyes tight and . . . KISSED HER. When he opened them again, there stood the most beautiful princess he had ever seen.

Prince Wilfred fell in love with her at once, and they were married the next day. The princess kept her promise and helped Prince Wilfred with his sums. She even taught him to say his two times table - backwards!

16 Mrs Porter's Daughter

Mrs Porter had a daughter
Who just loved to play with water,
And, one evening, for a laugh
Turned both taps on in the bath.
How the water overflowed!
Through the house and down the road -
Swept her daughter out to sea
Off to France and Italy.
But when her daughter got to Spain,
She was never seen again.
Said a tearful Mrs Porter,
"What a dreadful waste of water!"

17 The Marvellous Marrow

Mr Chippy loved gardening. One day while he was weeding his onions, he noticed a marrow growing on the compost heap. I don't remember planting that, thought Mr Chippy. But from then on he watered the plant every day.

The marrow grew l o n g e r and bigger and **fatter** until one Tuesday Mrs Chippy looked out of her cottage window and gasped.

"Look! That blooming marrow is enormous!"

And so it was.

"That marrow would make a good house," said Mr Chippy. "Our cottage is a bit small."

Mr Chippy put a door and some windows in the giant vegetable, and the Chippys moved in straightaway. But the neighbours started to complain.

"Your marrow spoils our view," they said. "Move it."

Now the Chippys had grown very fond of their marrow house, and the thought of losing it made them sad. So Mr Chippy fixed four big wheels to the marrow, put an engine at the front and made a steering wheel. When everything was ready Mr Chippy started up the engine, and Mrs Chippy chopped through the stalk.

"Off we go," they cried.

The Chippys were soon speeding along the motorway to the seaside. When they got there Mr Chippy looked out to sea.

"We could travel round the world," he said.

"There and back again," agreed Mrs Chippy.

So Mr Chippy made a sail, and turned the marrow into a boat. Mrs Chippy pushed it down the beach and into the sea. The marrow floated perfectly.

"What a marvellous marrow!" said the Chippys as they sailed away.

 The New Arrival

A new animal had arrived in Noah's Park. Some of the others had seen it, but nobody knew what it was. So they asked Noah if he knew.

"It's got two long legs at the back," said a monkey.

"And two short legs at the front," said Mrs Rabbit.

"It's got a big, thick tail," said an elephant.

"It's got a pocket in its tummy!" said a lion.

"And it can hop, like me," said a frog.

Noah scratched his head and thought for a moment.

"I wonder what animal that could be?" he said. "Let me see. It has two long legs at the back; two short ones at the front; a thick tail; it's got a pocket in its tummy and . . ."

Just then the new animal came hopping along.

"It's . . . a KANGAROO!" said Noah.

He was right.

"Hello," said the kangaroo.

"Welcome to the Park!" said Noah.

"Now we know who you are."

Pretending

We're playing at doctors and nurses –
Austin has got a bad leg.
"I may have to cut it off with my saw,"
Says Melanie, shaking her head.

Edward says, "Look. I'm a dentist.
Here's a tooth that will have to come out.
You won't feel a thing, I'll pull it with string. . .
Open wide and stop wriggling about!"

 Speckly Hen

Speckly Hen lives in a barn
Lays her eggs all over the farm.

One in the meadow,

Two in the trees,

Three by the hive and the honeybees.

Four by the duckpond,

Five on a mat,

Six in the farmer's old green hat!

Things That Float and Some That Don't

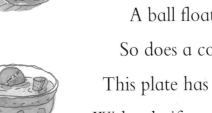

Boats float,

Stones sink,

My shoe floats . . . I think.

A ball floats,

So does a cork.

This plate has sunk,

With a knife and fork.

My shoe *was* floating,

But now it's . . . sinking.

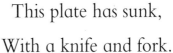

It's sinking,

It's sinking.

Please, Miss, my shoe is sinking!

The Blue Moon

It was the middle of the day and the little monsters, Meeny, Miny and Mo were going to bed. Everyone sleeps by day on Pongo and wakes up at night. The moon shone brightly that day. It was so light the little monsters couldn't get to sleep.

"We must do something about that moon," they said.

So they went outside. They found a pot of paint and some brushes, and fetched a long ladder. It reached all the way to the moon.

"Up we go!" said Meeny.

The ladder shook as the little monsters started to climb. Up and up and up. It took quite a time to get to the top, but at last they were standing on the moon.

Then Meeny, Miny and Mo got busy with their paintbrushes. They painted the moon BLUE! When they had finished, a pale shadowy light shone down on Pongo.

"That's better!" said Miny and Mo.

But by the time they had all climbed down again, it was night time . . . and the sun was shining.

So the little monsters didn't go to sleep after all.

23 Shop, shop, shopping

When Mum goes shopping
There's just no stopping
With the shop, shop, shopping.
We buy;
Hats, mats
This and thats
A watering can
Gloves for Gran
Shorts, shirts
Pants and vest
Party shoes to keep for best
Material for Mum's new dress
Finger paints to make a mess
A puzzle, too
For me to do
A potted plant –
That's for Aunt,
Some bread and cakes . . .
For goodness sakes!

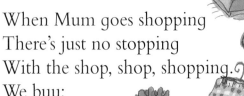

PLEASE!
No more shopping
We're drop, drop, dropping
All the shop, shop, shopping!

24 Forgotten

I've been to dancing class today
And now it's time for home
Everybody else has gone
But I am here alone.

I'm waiting and I'm waiting
I'm waiting by the door.
I'm sure I've been forgotten –
It's nearly *half-past-four*.

My dancing teacher says she's sure
That Mummy won't be long.
She's never been this late before –
Something must be wrong.

I'm waiting and I'm waiting
I'm waiting by the gate.
I'm sure I've been forgotten –
It's getting very late . . .

But then I hear a squeal of tyres
A car door slams outside
And Mummy's running up the path,
Her arms are open wide.
"My darling, I AM sorry,
Oh, my precious little lamb,
Of course you weren't forgotten –
You could NEVER be forgotten.
I was in a traffic jam!"

25 Autumn Leaves

Mr Bear is in his garden today. The wind has blown leaves all over the lawn.

"I must sweep those up," says Mr Bear.

"I'll help," says Little Bear.

So Mr Bear sweeps the leaves into a tidy pile, and Little Bear puts them into a wheelbarrow. Suddenly, a gust of wind blows all the leaves into the air, and they fly round and round.

"Oh dear!" says Mr Bear. "All that work for nothing."

Little Bear has an idea. He runs off to find his fishing net.

"Look!" he says, "I'll catch them in this."

Mr Bear laughs as Little Bear runs round the garden, chasing leaves with his net. He catches a few, but most of them fly out of reach.

"I've got a better idea," says Mr Bear.

He goes to the shed and fetches Little Bear's kite.

"Let's go to the park and fly your kite," he says. "We can sweep those leaves some other time."

"Ooo, yes!" says Little Bear. "That's the best thing to do on a windy day!"

26 Bugs, bugs, bugs

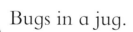
Bugs in a jug.

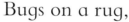
Bugs on a rug,

Bugs in the bed,
Bugs round my head.

Bugs in the park,
Bugs in the dark.

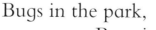

Bugs out at sea,

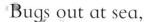

Bugs having tea . . .

Bug everybody but
don't bug ME!

27 Crafty Fox and Mother Hen

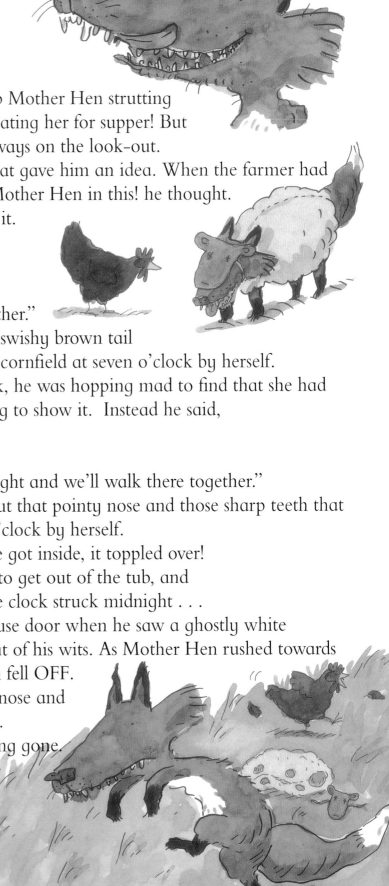

Crafty Fox loved to eat chicken. He often watched plump Mother Hen strutting about the farmyard. His mouth watered at the thought of eating her for supper! But he knew catching her wouldn't be easy. The farmer was always on the look-out.

Then Crafty Fox saw the farmer shearing sheep - and that gave him an idea. When the farmer had finished work, he stole a sheepskin and put it on. I'll fool Mother Hen in this! he thought.

He knocked on the henhouse door. Mother Hen opened it.

"I know where there is some ripe corn," said Crafty Fox.

"Where?" asked Mother Hen.

"In the big field over the hill," said Crafty Fox. "I'll call for you at eight o'clock, and we'll walk there together."

Mother Hen agreed but there was something about that swishy brown tail that didn't seem quite right for a sheep. So she went to the cornfield at seven o'clock by herself.

When Crafty Fox came to the henhouse at eight o'clock, he was hopping mad to find that she had been there and back already. But he was much too cunning to show it. Instead he said,

"I know where there is a tub of oatmeal."

"Where?" asked Mother Hen.

"In the barn," said Crafty Fox. "I'll call for you at midnight and we'll walk there together."

Again Mother Hen agreed but there was something about that pointy nose and those sharp teeth that didn't seem quite right. So she went to the barn at eleven o'clock by herself.

Sure enough she found the tub of oatmeal. But when she got inside, it toppled over! Mother Hen flapped and squawked. It took her some time to get out of the tub, and she was covered in floury oatmeal. She hurried home as the clock struck midnight . . .

Meanwhile Crafty Fox was just knocking on the henhouse door when he saw a ghostly white creature flapping across the farmyard. It frightened him out of his wits. As Mother Hen rushed towards the henhouse, Crafty Fox leaped aside - and the sheepskin fell OFF.

Then Mother Hen saw his swishy brown tail, his pointy nose and his sharp teeth . . . and she SCREECHED the place down.

Her squawking woke the farmer, but Crafty Fox was long gone. He ran over the hills, and was never seen again. As for Mother Hen - she has never trusted another sheep to this day.

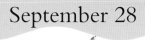

28 Dot and Doris

It was September. Dot was gathering nuts and berries in the wood. As she scuttled among the trees, she sniffed the air. Winter will be here soon, thought Dot. I must store up lots of food!

In a while she met her friend Doris lazing in the sun.

"You work too hard," said Doris. "Come and sit with me."

"I've got to collect acorns and rose-hips now," said Dot, "or I will have nothing to eat in winter."

"Oh, there's plenty of time for that," said Doris, dozing off again.

The days went by. Golden brown leaves fell from the trees and soon the branches were bare. A cold wind blew through the woods, and autumn turned to winter.

One frosty evening Doris felt very hungry. She ran along the hedgerow, searching among roots and brambles for something to eat. But there wasn't a nut or a berry to be found.

"*Too late, too late, t-ooooo late!*" hooted an owl.

Meanwhile Dot was snug in her hole. She was just going to sleep, when she heard a *tap-tap-tapping* at the door. She got out of bed and opened it.

Doris was on the doorstep, looking very sorry for herself.

"I'm hungry!" she said. "I've been a very silly mouse."

So Dot invited Doris in and gave her a good supper.

Later that evening Dot said,

"I have enough food for both of us. You can stay with me."

"Thank you," said Doris. "You are a good friend."

Then the two mice curled up and went to sleep all winter.

Rush Hour

D*rrring-drrring!* The alarm clock by Mr and Mrs Pig's bed goes off at **eight o'clock**.

Mr Pig is still snoring, so Mrs Pig wakes him up.

Mr Pig goes downstairs to make a cup of tea. Or, rather he *falls* downstairs, because Potter Pig has left his roller skates in a silly place at the top.

"Just wait 'til I see Potter!" says Mr Pig rubbing his sore nose.

Mrs Pig wakes Potter and the piglets. Then everyone wants to go to the bathroom at once.

"Hurry up!" shouts Mrs Pig, "and don't forget to wash your ears."

At a **quarter-past eight** Mr Pig carries the tea-tray upstairs. But oh dear! He has forgotten about Potter's roller skates which have rolled half-way down . . . and he trips over them *again*.

Meanwhile Potter has put on his new school uniform, and Mrs Pig is helping the piglets tie their shoelaces.

At **half-past eight** Mrs Pig makes breakfast. Potter and the piglets eat bowls of hot porridge. *Slurp, slurp, slurp.* Breakfast time with the Pig Family is quite noisy.

After that there is just enough time to kiss everyone goodbye, before Mr Pig has to catch his train to work. Kiss, kiss, kiss, for the three piglets. A kiss for Potter, and a big kiss for Mrs Pig. Then Mr Pig runs all the way to the railway station.

At **a quarter-to-nine** Mrs Pig, Potter and the piglets put on their coats, and walk to school. First, Mrs Pig takes the piglets to Nursery School.

"See you at lunchtime," she says.

Next she takes Potter to the Big School nearby.

"See you at teatime," says Mrs Pig.

Mrs Pig looks at her watch.

"I've got five minutes to get to work!" she says.

So Mrs Pig hurries down the road to the shop, where she sells books.

And, **at nine o'clock sharp**, she is ready for her customers.

Phew! thinks Mrs Pig. It's amazing what you can do in an hour.

30 Doctor Dog's Special Day

Doctor Dog wakes up early. He has a feeling *something* important is happening today, but he can't think what. While he is having breakfast, the postman arrives.

"You've got a lot of post this morning," he says.

Doctor Dog takes his letters but, he puts them in the fridge!

He wanders into the garden trying to remember what is so special about today. He notices a hole in the fence.

"Perhaps I'm supposed to be mending my fence," says Doctor Dog. "I'll get a hammer and fix it."

He is busy working, when Nurse Kitty pedals by on her bicycle.

"See you at three o'clock," she calls out cheerfully.

"Er . . . will you?" says Doctor Dog.

Then Mrs Elephant comes along.

"See you at three o'clock," she trumpets.

Doctor Dog wants to ask Mrs Elephant what it's all about. It's a puzzle. He can't remember arranging to meet Nurse Kitty or Mrs Elephant, and he spends the rest of the morning worrying about it.

At lunchtime, Doctor Dog goes to the fridge and discovers the letters he put there by mistake.

"Silly me!" he says, quickly opening the envelopes. And, to his great surprise, he finds they all have birthday cards inside.

"*Now* I remember," says Doctor Dog, "it's my BIRTHDAY!"

Just then there is a knock at the door. There is Nurse Kitty, Mrs Elephant and lots of his friends on the doorstep.

"You invited us to your party today," says Nurse Kitty. "Don't you remember?"

"I'm afraid I forgot," he says.

"Never mind," says Nurse Kitty. "I've baked a cake."

"And I've made lots of jellies," says Mrs Elephant.

In fact everyone has brought something for the party, so they all have a wonderful time.

"This is one birthday," says Doctor Dog, "I shall never forget!"

1 There's a Shark in Our Pond

"There's a shark in our pond!" cried Jake.
"He looks very hungry to me."
"Don't talk rubbish," said Dad.
"Hurry up and get on with your tea."

"He's swallowed our cat!" cried Jake.
"And now he's licking his lips,
His head's poking through our front window -
He's eating my sausage and chips."

Then Dad came in from the kitchen,
To have a quick word with his son.
There was Jake's empty plate on the table -
But Jake and the shark . . . had gone.

2 My New Umbrella

I've put my new umbrella up
To keep me from the rain,
But if the sun comes shining through . . .
I'll put it down again!

3 Autumn Friends

Woodmouse,
Squirrel,
Pheasant,
Vole;
Red fox,
Hedgehog,
Song thrush,
Mole.
Frog by the water,
Snail on the wall -
Look and name these autumn friends;
Did you find them all?

4 Little Bear's Toffee Apples

Thump! Thump! Thump!

Apples are falling from Mrs Bear's apple tree today.

"Let's get a basket and pick them up," she says to Little Bear.

So Little Bear fetches a basket, and they collect the fruit.

Afterwards Little Bear helps Mrs Bear make an apple cake and some pies. But there are still three apples left over.

"I know," says Little Bear. "We could make toffee apples."

"Good idea," says Mrs Bear. "We'll need lots of sugar for the toffee."

Little Bear weighs out the sugar and puts it in a pan. Mrs Bear adds a squeeze of lemon and some water, and puts it on the stove to heat. Soon the mixture is bubbling hot.

"*Mmmm!*" says Little Bear. "It smells scrummy."

While Mrs Bear stirs the toffee, Little Bear washes and dries the apples. Then he puts them on a plate, and pushes a wooden stick through each one.

When they are ready, Little Bear dips the apples one by one into the pan. He twirls them round in the mixture until they are covered in sticky toffee.

"Mind your paws," warns Mrs Bear. "The toffee is still very hot."

Little Bear puts them on a buttered plate to cool. When the toffee is hard, there is a delicious sugary brown apple for Mr Bear, Mrs Bear and for Little Bear who made them.

Crunch!

Crunch!

Crunch!

5 Keys please, Louise!

Whenever Louise's mum went out she'd say, "Keys please, Louise!" and Louise would go to the key holder in the kitchen and fetch the right key. There was a key for the front door, the back door and one for the garden shed. The car keys were always on the last little hook at the end.

One morning Mum was in a hurry to drive Louise to school.

"Keys please, Louise!" said Mum.

Louise ran to get them but the car keys were missing.

"They're not here," she shouted.

"They must be," said Mum.

Louise looked again but the car keys weren't there. Mum frowned and hunted round for them. Louise helped too. She searched by the telephone, under a chair and even in the waste paper basket.

Meanwhile Mum was busily emptying her bag on to the table. Amongst the jumble of things was her purse, two toffees, a lipstick, one comb and a ticket from the dry cleaners – but no car keys.

Louise looked at her mum. She was wearing her favourite jacket with big pockets.

"Have you looked in your pockets, Mum?" she asked.

"Well, no," said Mum, suddenly rummaging in both pockets at once. And, to her great surprise – the keys were in one of them.

"What a noodle!" said Mum, giving Louise a hug. "I remember now. I collected this jacket from the cleaners yesterday, and wore it home. I must have slipped the keys in my pocket."

From then on Mum always tried to put her keys back on the hook, which saved them both a lot of trouble.

"Keys please, Louise!"

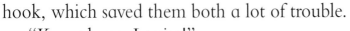

Be dotty and say this quickly

6 Dotty Dinosaur

Dotty was a dinosaur
With prehistoric spots;
The dottiest sight you ever saw
Was Dotty's spotty dots.
Be dotty and say this quickly.

7 The Wolf as Big as an Elephant

There was once a farmer who had a lazy son called Kevin. Although the boy was useless at work, he was good at telling stories.

One harvest time Kevin's dad said,

"Stack the hay in the barn, before the rain comes."

Kevin lifted a few bales but it was hard work. So he thought of an excuse to stop. He ran to his dad shouting,

"There's a wolf in the barn, big as an ELEPHANT!"

"A wolf as big as an elephant?" said Dad. "I don't think so."

"I meant as big as a BABY ELEPHANT," said Kevin.

"A wolf as big as a baby elephant?" Dad said. "I don't think so."

"Well, maybe not but it was as big as a LION." said Kevin.

"A wolf as big as a lion?" said Dad. "I don't think so."

"Well, it was certainly as big as a COW," said Kevin.

"A wolf as big as a cow?" said Dad. "I don't think so."

Kevin thought for a moment.

"Well, it was big as a CAT," he said.

"A wolf as big as a cat?" said Dad. "I don't think so."

"I meant as big as a KITTEN," said Kevin.

"A wolf as big as a kitten?" said Dad. "I don't think so."

"Well," said Kevin, "it was certainly as big as a MOUSE."

"Hm? A wolf as big as a mouse?" said Dad "I don't think so! I've heard enough of this silly story, Kevin. Now, stack that hay in the barn!"

8 Bathroom Nonsense

Wash your hair with custard,
Scrub your face with ink,
Clean your teeth with cream cheese . . .
Then go to bed in the sink!

9 Making Music

Trill! goes the trumpet,

Twang! goes the harp,

Peep! goes the piccolo, shrill and sharp.

Clash! go the cymbals,

Clang! go the chimes,

Boom! goes the bass drum, umpteen times!

10 Five Brown Cows

Five brown cows on a green hill, grazing,
Four white swans over blue seas, flying,
Three grey donkeys on yellow straw, standing,
Two ginger kittens by a red fire, sleeping,
One black rat with a pink nose, twitching.

11 Mr Star's Car

Mr Star bought a car,
Drove it proudly near and far.

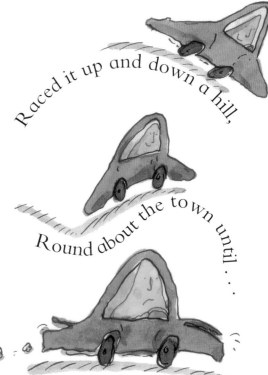

Raced it up and down a hill,

Round about the town until . . .

Splutter, splutter, hiss, bang, pop!
The car came to a sudden stop.

"What's the matter, little car?"
Said a worried Mr Star.

Said the car, "Well, can't you see?
I'm out of petrol. Please FILL me!"

12 A Thimble Too Much

The dolls, Elizabeth and Rebecca, were moving house. Teddy and Robot were helping to load furniture into a toy removal van. There were so many things!

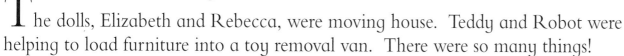

They loaded two beds, a sofa, a big armchair, a rocking chair,

a chest of drawers, a grandfather clock, a wardrobe, the kitchen table . . .

and all the pots and pans.

"Phew!" said Teddy, "I'm puffed."

"There's still more," said Robot, "and the van is nearly full."

"Don't forget my dresses, please," said Elizabeth.

"Or my hats and shoes!" said Rebecca.

"We'll bring the sewing machine and workbasket," said the dolls.

Teddy and Robot managed to squeeze everything in. The van was bulging at the sides.

"What a load," said Teddy.

"I'll drive," said Robot.

He was just going to start the engine when Rebecca came running out of the doll's house. She was holding a tiny thimble.

"I nearly left this behind," she said, and popped the thimble inside.

But oh, dear! The load was just too heavy. The van tipped over backwards and everything fell out.

"It was the thimble that did it," said Teddy.

"Now we'll have to start all over again," said Robot.

"This time," said Rebecca, "I'll carry that thimble myself!"

213

13 Sophie Goes to Dream Island

"Sweet dreams," said Sophie's mum at bedtime one night.

I wonder where dreams come from? thought Sophie sleepily. She was still thinking when her magic bed whispered,

"Left, right, hold on tight.
We're off to the Land of Dreams tonight."

The bed whirled once round the bedroom and out of the window. Sophie hugged her teddies. Where were they going this time? The magic bed had taken her on so many exciting adventures. Right now they were sliding down a moonbeam.

They landed with a bump on an island.

"Here we are," said the bed. "Dream Island."

The bed took Sophie to meet a man called Mr Makebelieve. He was tinkering with a strange-looking machine.

"What's that?" asked Sophie.

"It's a Dream Machine," said Mr Makebelieve.

"Does it really make dreams?" said Sophie.

"Of course," he said. "What sort of dream would you like?"

Sophie looked at the dials. There were so many dreams to choose from - wild dreams, daydreams, nightmares, forty winks . . .

"May I have a sweet dream?" she said.

"Good choice," said Mr Makebelieve.

He pressed a button and the machine made a loud whirring noise. Suddenly Sophie found herself in an orchard. But it was no ordinary orchard. The trees were full of sweets!

Sophie could hardly believe her eyes. She ran from tree to tree picking toffees, chocolate bars and sparkling fizzy chews.

In a while Sophie heard a voice calling,

"Left, right, hold on tight.
Home again before morning light."

It was Sophie's bed, ready to take her home.

"All good dreams must come to an end," said Mr Makebelieve.

"It was one of the best dreams I've ever had," said Sophie. Then she climbed into bed and waved goodbye.

Next morning Mum said, "Did you sleep well, Sophie?"

Sophie told her mum about Dream Island.

"You must have been dreaming!" said Mum.

But when Sophie rubbed the sleep from her eyes, she saw something her mum hadn't noticed. There at the foot of the bed was - a sparkling fizzy chew!

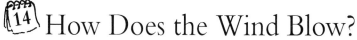 How Does the Wind Blow?

How does the breeze blow,
Rustling all the leaves so?
It goes *whispering* by.

How does the wind blow,
Blowing round the house so?
It goes *whistling* by.

How does the storm blow,
Tossing all the ships so?
It goes *roaring* by!

15 All Stuck Up

Mr Pig is busy wallpapering Potter's new bedroom. He brushes the gooey paste on to a strip of wallpaper, *Slap, slap, slap!*

"*Tum-te-ta, tum-te-toe,*" sings Mr Pig as he climbs the step-ladder with a bundle of sticky paper. At the top a fly lands on his nose. "Shoo!" he says.

The fly doesn't budge, so Mr Pig tries to blow it away. *Phoooof!* But the fly just sits there. And it tickles.

Mr Pig is balancing on the steps with his arms full of wallpaper. He lets go with one arm to swipe the fly . . . the ladder wobbles . . . Mr Pig wobbles . . . and topples off!

Bumperty-bumperty-bump he goes, knocking over the bucket of paste on his way down. The wallpaper goes flying and the bucket lands on his head.

"Help!" cries Mr Pig.

Potter comes to see what is the matter. The strip of wallpaper comes floating down, and wraps round Potter like a parcel. To make matters worse the piglets run in, and slip on the paste which has spilled all over the floor. They are having a wonderful time sliding when Mrs Pig comes to see what all the noise is about.

"What a mess!" she says.

Mr Pig explains about the fly which is now buzzing round the room. Mrs Pig looks cross as it flits past her nose. She rolls up some wallpaper and is about to swat it, when the fly zooms out of an open window.

"Good!" says Mrs Pig slamming the window shut. "That fly has caused quite enough trouble for one day!"

I Know a Tumbly House

I know a tumbly house
With a creaky little door,
Where a squeaky little mouse
Lives below a rotten floor.

Inside those crumbly walls
There's a musty little room,
Where a dusty little ghost
Hums a mournful little tune.

At least that's what I'm *told* is there,
So one day when I'm bold, I'll dare
To peep inside that spooky house
And see the ghost myself,

But not just yet . . .

October Morning

Bright sun dawning
On a damp, misty morning,
Farmer up and yawning
To milk the dairy cows.

And all along the hedgerow
Where berries, nuts and seeds grow,
Squirrels and field mice go
To gather winter stores.

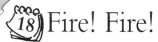

Fire! Fire!

"Fire! Fire!" says Jeremiah.
"Ring the bell," says Mrs Fell.
"Fetch some water," says her daughter.
"Make it quick!" says brother, Nick.
"Hold the hose," says Mr Rose.
"It's gone out," says Tommy Trout.
"So what was all the fuss about!"

Tuesdays

Tuesday,
A shopping for shoes day
Time I can choose day
Some shiny new shoes.

Tuesday,
A get up and do day
A come out with you day
To play in the park.

Tuesday,
A haven't a clue day
A stay home and snooze day
In front of the fire.

Tuesday,
Waiting in a queue day
To go to the zoo day . . .
The best day of all!

217

20 Fantastic Gymnastic!

Rachel does gymnastics
In a proper leotard,
With a badge she's been awarded
For working very hard
doing lots of

bends *and stretches,*

And for walking on a bar

Without wobbling or falling off –
She's quite a little star.
She can somersault and cartwheel;
Turn some roly-polys too,
And bounce upon a trampoline
The way that gymnasts do.
Says Rachel, "It's fantastic,
Since I've learnt to be gymnastic,

I'm as *stretchy as elastic!"*

21 A Prickly Problem

Doctor Dog and Nurse Kitty are visiting Mr Badger who lives in the woods. He has a bad cough. Doctor Dog listens to his chest with a stethoscope and Nurse Kitty gives him a bottle of cough syrup.

"You must take two large spoonfuls, twice a day," she says.

They are just leaving when Mr Badger hears someone sobbing outside his door. It's Baby Hedgehog.

"I've lost my mummy!" says the prickly baby.

Mr Badger wants to help but Doctor Dog says he must stay at home in the warm.

"We'll look for Mrs Hedgehog," he says.

Finding her is not easy because the woods are thick with leaves. They hunt around for a long time until Doctor Dog sits down to rest . . .

"OUCH!" he yells, leaping up again.

"Mummy!" says Baby Hedgehog running to meet her.

"Well done, Doctor Dog," says Nurse Kitty. "You found Mrs Hedgehog after all!"

22 Clap Your Hands

Clap your hands when I say one,
Clap your hands and wiggle your tongue.
Nod your head when I say two,
Nod your head and touch your shoe.
Stamp your foot when I say three,
Stamp your foot and touch your knee.
Bend right over when I say four,
Bend right over and touch the floor!

23 Noah Sends a Message

It was Noah's birthday on Saturday, and he wanted to invite all his friends to a party.

First he began by writing invitations. He would send one each to Flip and Flap, the penguins. Then there were the two little owls, Mrs Rabbit and her family, Mr and Mrs Emu, the monkeys, Mrs Green Grass Snake, the three bears . . .

Noah stopped. There were so many animals in the Park. It would take him a long time to write all those invitations, and how would he get them delivered in time?

Noah went into his garden to think. He looked up at the blue sky and saw one puffy little white cloud drifting overhead. And THAT gave him an idea. He hurried inside and painted his invitation in great big letters on . . . a sheet!

Then Noah asked some birds to fly it across the sky, so that all the animals could read his message:

Please come to my birthday Party at 3 o'clock on Saturday
Love, Noah x

Which is how everybody got to know about Noah's party, and they all had a wonderful time.

 24 It's Not Fair!

One day Katie's little brother, George, wasn't well. Ma Purrkins put him to bed and took his temperature. Pa Purrkins brought him a soothing drink. At bedtime Katie read him a story.

Next morning Katie had to get up early to go to school. Ma took George his breakfast in bed. Katie had to get her own breakfast.

When she came home from school, Granny Purrkins was there. She had brought George a get well present.

"It's not fair!" said Katie.

After tea Katie had to practise her lines for the school play while George sat up and watched television.

"It's not fair!" she said. "I wish I was ill."

"That's just silly," said Ma.

A week later George was better but Katie wasn't well. Ma put her to bed and took her temperature. Pa brought her a soothing drink and read her a story. George gave her his blanket to cuddle.

Next day she couldn't go to school. Ma brought her breakfast in bed. Pa took George to playschool. Granny Purrkins came to visit and brought Katie a present.

It was a long day and Katie was bored. She missed her friends. She had missed the dress rehearsal for the school play.

"It's not fair!" she said.

Soon Katie was well again. Mrs Tabby, the teacher, and all Katie's friends were very pleased to see her back at school.

"We were worried you would miss the play," they said. "Now *that* wouldn't be fair, would it?"

221

 When Mole Went Digging . . .

When Mole went digging under the town . . . first he found himself in a BASEMENT. The family living there weren't too pleased.

"Go and dig somewhere else," they said.

So Mole dug a bit further, round a corner and into a LIFT SHAFT. The lift had lots of people in it. Mole watched as it zoomed upwards.

"Lifts are not for me," he said.

Instead he tunnelled down and along until he found himself in a CAR PARK. There were rows and rows of cars parked underground.

Suddenly two bright headlights shone and a horn blared, *beep beep!*

"Out of the way!" shouted the driver.

Mole didn't wait a second longer. He dug furiously until, he came to a BIG TUNNEL. Mole ran along it until he came to a STATION. It was crowded with passengers, waiting on the platform.

As Mole squeezed between them, he felt a rush of air coming through the tunnel. Then, *whooosh!* a TUBE TRAIN came racing along the rails and stopped.

"Mind the doors!" said a voice over the loudspeaker.

Mole was pushed into a carriage. Then they were off, speeding through another tunnel to the next station. When the train stopped again, Mole got off quickly.

"It's all so busy down here," he said.

By now Mole was hoping to find somewhere quiet to snooze. He was digging away when he came to a SEWER. Mole was swept off his feet by a river of dirty water. It swirled its way along more tunnels until, Mole got caught in a DRAIN.

He hoisted himself up through the grille. His pink nose twitched as he ran along a ditch and into a GARDEN.

"At last!" said Mole, digging one more tunnel which was full of . . . WORMS. "I'll have my supper then go to sleep."

26 Three Out Walking

When Hamish MacGregor and I go out
Titus, my cat, comes too.
We walk in a line
He complains all the time -
The way that some cats do.

Hamish MacGregor keeps stopping to sniff,
Tracking the scent of a beast.
Wagging his tail,
He's hot on the trail
Of a lion . . . or a beetle at least.

Hamish MacGregor is always behind,
Titus likes striding ahead;
And, hey diddle diddle
I'm in the middle
Taking them home to be fed.

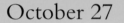

27 The No Such Ghost

There was once a little ghost who lived in an old house. An artist called Holly lived there too.

Every day Holly painted pictures in her studio, near the attic. It was a bit creepy up there but when visitors asked, "Do you have a ghost in this old house?" Holly would say, "There's no such thing." The little ghost had heard this so often, he thought No Such Thing was his name.

No Such Thing loved to watch Holly at work, painting pictures for books. Because No Such Thing was invisible, Holly never *knew* the little ghost was there - even when he looked over her shoulder!

One morning while No Such Thing was floating about the studio, Holly looked puzzled. She had been asked to draw the pictures for a ghost story. I've never seen a ghost before, thought Holly. I wonder what they look like?

Of course No Such Thing knew what Holly was thinking and wanted to help. He flew to her easel and did cartwheels all over her paper. Holly shivered. She felt a cold draught as the little ghost did his best to show himself. But she couldn't see him.

Then No Such Thing did something quite extraordinary. He took a pencil - and drew a picture of himself. After all, only a ghost knows what he looks like. Holly couldn't believe her eyes. The pencil was drawing all by itself! Before long, there was a perfect picture of a ghost, smiling up at her. Underneath the little ghost had written;

> *This is a picture of me.*
> *With love from,*
> *No Such Thing*

From that day, whenever anyone asked Holly if she had a ghost in the house, she would smile over her shoulder and say, "There's . . .
No Such Thing." And she meant it.

28 Roger the Robot

Roger is a robot
With tinny hands and feet,
A super brain and saucer ears
Makes Roger quite complete.
Though he's supersonic clever
And can speak with metal lips –
All he eats for breakfast
Is a bowl of micro chips!

29 Green-eyed Witches

Down in the woods where the trees are bare
And twigs scritch scratch to tangle your hair,
There in the light of a sliver of moon
The green-eyed witches sit and croon
In tattered capes and pointed hats
Around a cauldron filled with bats.
They fly on broomsticks way up high
To sweep dark cobwebs from the sky,
And catch giant spiders for a brew . . .
At Halloween – they might snatch you!

30 A Scary Year

January giants are big and smelly
February beasts slurp slime green jelly
March mad monsters stomp their feet
April trolls dig worms to eat
May bugs nip your nose and toes
June bad gremlins grab your clothes
July vampires bite at night
August ghosts are spooky white
September skeletons dance and clatter
October witches fry toads in batter
November gnomes are a scary bunch
December ogres crunch kids for lunch
So be very careful all year through . . .
or one of these beasties might catch **YOU!**

gooey
Slime

📅31 Ben's Halloween Party

It was Halloween and Ben was having a fancy dress party. His friend, Joshua was helping to get things ready. They began by making a lantern out of a fat pumpkin.

"I'll cut the top off for you," said Ben's dad. "It's tough and needs a sharp knife."

When that was done the boys had fun scooping out the inside with spoons. They scooped out a lot of pumpkin!

"I can make a pie with some of that," said Ben's mum.

Then Ben and Joshua cut out shapes to make a grinning face, and Dad gave them a 'nite-light' candle to put inside.

"We'll light it later," he said.

"Can we put our costumes on now?" asked Ben.

"Yes," said Mum, "but I think I'd better help with the face paint."

So Ben put on his skeleton suit and Mum painted his face white, with hollow black eyes. Joshua dressed up as a ghost, and Ben's mum gave him a ghostly green face.

"You look really scary," said Ben.

"Whoooooo-arrrrh!" moaned Joshua.

Just before the party, Dad helped Ben light the lantern and put it in the window. The pumpkin glowed bright orange in the dark. And at five o'clock Ben's other friends arrived.

There were three witches, one dragon, two vampires and a witch's cat. They played games and ate monster burgers for tea. Afterwards Dad turned out the lights and read spooky stories.

At bedtime that night Ben said, "That was the best party ever!"

"I'm glad you liked it," said Mum and kissed him goodnight.

"The ghost stories were great . . ." said Ben yawning.

"They were *just* stories," said Dad. "Now, go to sleep."

Ben closed his eyes. Downstairs the pumpkin lantern flickered and went out. Halloween was over for another year.

1 The Emperor's Moustache

Emperor Ho Hum was a fussy man. He spent his time fussing about little things. For instance at breakfast he counted the rice pops in his bowl. If there was one rice pop too many or, one too few, he complained to the cook. Or if he found one bent blade of grass in the garden, he got angry with the gardener. Silly old fusspot!

But there was one thing Ho Hum was particularly fussy about - his moustache. It was so long, it reached his toes.

Now Ho Hum had a servant called Ping Pong. It was his job to comb the emperor's moustache every day. And because Ho Hum insisted that both the left and right sides should have exactly the same number of hairs, Ping Pong was always counting them to make sure.

One evening Ho Hum was getting ready for a very important banquet. He put on his finest robes. Then he sat and looked at himself in the mirror.

Everything looked just right except . . . his moustache. He was sure one hair was missing!

"PING PONG!" he shouted. "Find that hair, or there'll be trouble."

Ping Pong got busy straightaway. "One, two, three . . ." Slowly he counted the hairs on the right. He made it SIXTY-ONE.

The emperor dozed off.

Ping Pong counted up on the left. But there were only SIXTY! What could he do? Even if I find the hair, he thought, I can't stick it back on. I must do something quickly.

So Ping Pong took a pair of scissors and . . .

Snip! He cut one hair OFF!

Just then Ho Hum woke up and looked in the mirror.

"You found it!" he said.

Ping Pong held the scissors firmly behind his back.

"There are exactly SIXTY hairs on both sides," he said truthfully.

"Well, since you are so clever," said Ho Hum, "I will make you my Chancellor."

Then they both went to the banquet together.

Just think. All that fuss about nothing!

Nobody Wants Me

Nobody wants me
I'm leaving home.
I'll be like a hermit
And live on my own.

I could sleep in a tent
In a dry desert land,
And ride on a camel
Across the hot sand.

I could go to the North Pole
To live on the ice,
And play with a polar bear -
That would be nice!

Or find a deep jungle
And live in a tree,
With parrots and monkeys
I'm sure they'd like me . . .

But wait,

Someone's calling
I've got to go home.
Somebody wants me
I *can't* live alone.

There's Mum and my Dad and
My sister, makes three.
I really would miss them -
And they would MISS ME!

(3) The Baker Man

Do you know the baker man?
He bakes bread as fast as he can.
Flour, water, yeast and so -
That's the way he makes the dough.

For;

long loaves,

short loaves,

big and small,

square or round,

He makes them all.

French bread,

wholemeal,

white and brown,

Bread for people in our town.

4 Got You!

Grandpa Bear has come to stay. He unpacks his things in the spare bedroom. Little Bear peeps round the door.

"Can't see me, Grandpa," he says.

"Oh, yes I can," says Grandpa.

"I've got eyes in the back of my head."

"No you haven't," says Little Bear.

"Oh, yes I have," says Grandpa.

"Where am I, then?" says Little Bear.

"You're hiding behind the door," says Grandpa.

"Where am I now?" says Little Bear.

"You're creeping up behind me," says Grandpa.

"You can't catch me," says Little Bear.

"I don't want to," says Grandpa.

"You couldn't catch me, even if you wanted to," says Little Bear.

"If I *did* want to," says Grandpa, "I could."

"If I called you Grandbaggie, would you want to?" says Little Bear.

"I *might*," says Grandpa.

"What if I called you Grandbaggie Shaggy Ears?" says Little Bear.

"Well . . . if you called me *that*, I'd want to catch you," says Grandpa.

"Grandbaggie Shaggy . . ."

"GOT YOU!" says Grandpa.

And he hugged Little Bear to pieces.

5 Bonfire Night

Wrap up warm,
Snug and tight.
We're going out
It's Bonfire Night.

The flames are hot
Our faces glow,
Waiting for the
The firework show.

BANG! they're off
And way up high
A million stars
Burst in the sky.

6 Matching Socks

Sort these socks in pairs;
The zebras and bears
The spots and the stripes
The red, green and whites
The long and the shorts
The thick ones for sports
Put the patterned and plain
Back together again.
Match each sock here -
So they're ready to wear!

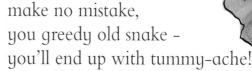

7 Algy the Snake

When he's awake,
Algy, the snake
is all bumps and bulges
because he indulges
in buckets of custard
hotdogs and mustard,
spaghetti in sauce,
a cow and a horse,
sugary pancakes
fried chips and steaks
and, just for luck,
a hen and a duck . . .

make no mistake,
you greedy old snake -
you'll end up with tummy-ache!

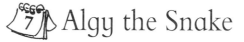

231

8 Ali Baa Baa

One evening Ali Baa Baa, the ram, was eating grass. Suddenly he looked up and saw the sun slip behind the mountain.

"Crumpling horns!" said Ali Baa Baa. "I must go and tell my wife the sun is falling."

So Ali Baa Baa went to his wife, Curly-Whirly.

"Curly-Whirly," cried Ali Baa Baa, "the sun is falling."

"Great balls of wool!" cried Curly-Whirly. "We must go and tell the cow who lives in the meadow."

So Ali Baa Baa and Curly-Whirly went to see the cow, Cooey-Mooey. It was midnight when they got to the meadow.

"Cooey-Mooey," cried Ali Baa Baa, "the sun is falling."

"Fizzling milkshakes!" cried Cooey-Mooey. "We must go and tell the horse who lives in the farmyard."

So Ali Baa Baa, Curly-Whirly and Cooey-Mooey went along to see the horse, Clippy-Cloppy.

It was nearly dawn when they got to the farmyard.

"Clippy-Cloppy," cried Ali Baa Baa, "the sun is falling."

"Jumping haystacks!" cried Clippy-Cloppy. "We must go and tell the farmer."

So Ali Baa Baa, Curly-Whirly, Cooey-Mooey and Clippy-Cloppy all went to see the farmer, Deary Me.

"Deary Me," cried Ali Baa Baa, "the sun is falling."

Deary Me put her hands on her hips and laughed.

"Look behind you," she said. "The sun isn't falling . . . it's RISING."

Ali Baa Baa, Curly-Whirly, Cooey-Mooey and Clippy-Cloppy all looked. Sure enough, the sun was just coming up over the hill.

"Well, I'm glad about that," said Ali Baa Baa. "Now we can all go home!"

9 Globe Trotting

Rushing off to Russia,
Skipping down to France,
Hopping round America
If I have half a chance.
Popping into Africa, India and then
China and Australia,
There and back again!

11 Helping Hands

Wash the dishes,
Dry the dishes,
Put them all away.
We're helping with the washing-up
Before we go to play.

10 Never Say Can't

"Never say CAN'T,"
said little Duck's aunt.
"Take off and fly –
You CAN if you try.
Can't just won't do."

So Duck DID . . . and he flew!

12 Mr Malvolio's Magnificent Circus

Pearl loved books. One afternoon she found a new book on the library shelf. It was called *Mr Malvolio's Magnificent Circus*.

"You'll like that one," said Ruth, the librarian.

Pearl sat on the floor and opened it. She turned the first page. It was as if she were stepping right inside a gigantic tent. It was all so *real* - she could smell the sawdust, and hear the horses' hooves, thudding round the ring. A brass band was playing some lively music.

Whether Pearl got smaller or the book got bigger, I am not sure, but she found herself sitting in the audience watching the ringmaster, the great Mr Malvolio himself. He looked straight at Pearl.

"Welcome to my magnificent show," he said.

Next there was a roll of drums and a troupe of acrobats came cartwheeling into the ring. As quick as monkeys they climbed up ropes to a trapeze high overhead. Pearl gasped as the 'catcher' hung by his knees and swung backwards and forwards. Suddenly another acrobat leaped off her trapeze, turned a double somersault and flew to the catcher. Everyone clapped and cheered as he caught her.

No sooner was that over, when there was a loud *BANG!* The clowns had arrived in an old car. The doors fell off and the engine blew up, squirting water everywhere.

Pearl laughed as she watched the clowns having a tea party. She ducked just in time as a large and very creamy cake came flying into the audience . . .

Pearl went sprawling on the library floor.

"That was fun!" she said.

"I thought you'd enjoy reading that book," said Ruth.

And do you know, as Pearl put *Mr Malvolio's Magnificent Circus* back on the shelf - the tiniest specks of sawdust fell out. Fancy that.

13 Katie Goes Missing

One Saturday afternoon Ma Purrkins took Katie and George to Katkins Department Store. It was crowded with shoppers. Ma held tightly on to George and told Katie to keep by her side.

"We'll take the escalator to the Second Floor," said Ma. "I want to choose some new curtains."

It happened that the toy department was on the Second Floor too.

"Ooo, toys!" said George.

"Can we look at them?" asked Katie.

"Later," said Ma.

Ma took a long time choosing curtains. Katie waited and was soon bored. She really *did* want to look at the toys. So she wandered off ON HER OWN.

It was busier in the toy department than anywhere else. At first Katie didn't mind getting jostled. She was enjoying herself until someone trod on her tail.

"Ouch!" she cried.

At that moment Katie wanted Ma and George very badly. She was alone and felt a bit afraid. She squeezed past the pedal cars and tricycles looking for them. She peered round a big display of teddies. And just when she thought she'd NEVER find them . . . Katie heard a voice calling,

"KATIE! KATIE!"

It was George, sitting up high on Ma's shoulder. Katie ran and hugged Ma tight.

"Oh, Katie!" she scolded. "I've been so worried about you."

"I'm sorry," said Katie.

"Now," said Ma, "I've finished my shopping. Let's look at the toys *together*, then we'll go home for tea."

4 Musical Pigs

This little pig plays the piano
This little pig likes to hum
This little pig blows the tuba
This little pig bangs the drum . . .
And *that* little pig went, "Wee wee wee – I've just hit my thumb!"

📅15 Mr Rabbit's New Glasses

Nurse Kitty is in Mr Rabbit's shop buying some groceries.

"Good morning," she says. "Please may I have a packet of cornflakes and a pot of fishpaste?"

After a long time looking along the shelves, Mr Rabbit gives Nurse Kitty a box of soap flakes and a tin of soup.

"These are not what I asked for," she says.

"Oh dear," says Mr Rabbit. "My eyesight *is* a bit fuzzy."

Nurse Kitty helps him find the right things. Then she says, "I'm sure Doctor Dog could help you. Come to the surgery this afternoon."

So Mr Rabbit goes to see Doctor Dog.

"Just sit in this chair," he says. "I'll test your eyes."

Nurse Kitty holds up a picture for Mr Rabbit to look at.

"Can you see the carrots?" says Doctor Dog.

"What carrots?" says Mr Rabbit.

"Hm," says Doctor Dog. "I think you need some glasses."

Nurse Kitty goes to the cupboard and fetches a tray of spectacles. She gives Mr Rabbit a pair with shiny red frames.

"Try these," she says.

Mr Rabbit puts them on.

"Wow!" he says, hopping up and down. "I can see the carrots! I can see EVERYTHING! It doesn't look fuzzy anymore."

The next day Nurse Kitty goes to Mr Rabbit's shop. Mr Rabbit is behind the counter wearing his new glasses.

"I'd like some fish fingers today," she says.

And do you know? Mr Rabbit got it right first time!

16 Fine Pines

I
think
pine trees
are fine trees.
These tall, straight spires
give us poles for telephone wires!

18 Swing Me

Swing me high,
Swing me low,
Swing me over your shoulder.
Whizz me round like an aeroplane
Before I get any older.

17 My Tune

Bees may hum,
Birds may sing,
But I just whistle any old thing.

19 Little Miss Locket

Little Miss Locket, jumped in a rocket
The rocket blew up, so she rode in a cup
The cup had a crack, so she hopped in a sack
The sack was too loose, so she sat on a goose
The goose made a fuss, so she got on a bus
And spent all week at the TERMINUS.

 Just Thinking

One night Mr Bear was out walking near the Tum Tum tree. He stopped to look up at the moon.

"How AMAZING!" he said out loud.

At that moment Giraffe With a Scarf was passing. I wonder what's so special about the moon tonight? he thought. And he stopped to look at it.

Then Humpy Camel and Hee Haw Donkey came by. Little Cub was bounding along behind. When they saw Mr Bear and Giraffe With a Scarf, they stopped too.

"There must be something very strange about the moon tonight," they said. "Let's have a look."

After that Stripy Tiger joined them.

"There must be something extraordinary about the moon tonight," he said. "I must stay and see what it is."

They were all standing with Mr Bear, no one saying a word, when Police Constable Fox came along.

"What's going on?" he said.

Not one of them had a clue - except Mr Bear.

"I was just thinking," he said, "how AMAZING it would be if . . . the moon were made of *honey*. Just thinking. That's all."

Mr Bear continued with his walk. But he had started everyone thinking about what the moon was made of.

"It looks like hay to me," said Giraffe With a Scarf.

"No, its more like sand," said Humpy Camel.

"Porridge," said Hee Haw Donkey. "Definitely porridge."

"I think it's custard," said Little Cub, licking his lips.

"Or cream?" said Stripy Tiger.

But Police Constable Fox shook his head and said,

"Cheese, *that's* what it's made of. You can see the holes from here."

They all looked up. The moon with its craters was beaming down at them.

"You're right," said the others. "What a clever policeman you are!"

21 Whistle and Toot

Once there were two little dogs called Whistle and Toot. One day Whistle asked Toot to go for a walk with him.

"It's a fine day," he said. "There's not a cloud in the sky."

"There isn't one *now*," said Toot, "but there *might* be one later. I'll take my umbrella, just in case it rains."

The two friends set off. They hadn't gone far, when a gentle breeze blew round them. Toot looked worried.

"I think there's a storm coming," he said. "I'd better go home and fetch my coat and scarf, just in case." So Whistle waited while Toot went home. He came hurrying back, a little out of breath.

"Off we go," said Whistle. "I'll race you to the top of the hill."

But halfway up, Toot saw a tiny white cloud in the sky.

"Look," he said, "I'm sure it's going to snow. I'd better go home and fetch my hat and snow boots, just in case."

Toot ran all the way home for his hat and boots while Whistle sat and waited. It took some time before Toot returned, panting hard. He was weighed down with his umbrella, coat, scarf, hat and snow boots.

"I've done enough walking for one day," he said.

"That's because you worried about the weather too much," said Whistle. "It has stayed fine. It didn't rain. The storm didn't come, and it didn't snow. You've walked your paws off for nothing."

Toot had to laugh. But he ran all the way home, just in case . . .

22 Valerie

A little girl called Valerie
Went to a picture gallery.
Said Valerie, "I do not care
For any painting hanging there."
Whereupon she skipped off home
And drew some nice ones of her own.

📅23 Noah's Special Fire Brigade

One day Noah was tidying up his garden for the winter. He had lit a bonfire to burn the rubbish which, at first, made a lot of smoke. Then flames started leaping into the air. The bonfire was roaring away, when a sudden gust of wind fanned the flames – and Noah's hedge caught fire.

"Oh, my blooming gumboots!" cried Noah, as he ran to fetch some water.

When he got back, the fire had spread to some bushes and trees.

"I'll need lots of water to put this out," he said. "Help! Help!"

Some monkeys were the first to hear him. They came swinging through the trees, chattering nervously.

"Make a chain," said Noah.

So that's what they did. The monkeys stood in a line and handed buckets of water from the river to Noah. But it was *still* not enough.

Luckily Mrs Elephant came trumpeting along. She had seen the smoke, and had heard the fire crackling away.

"Please help," said Noah.

"Of course I will," she said.

So Mrs Elephant did something elephants do very well. She ran to the river, sucked up a whole trunkful of water and . . . SPLOOSH! squirted water on the fire, just like a hose on a fire engine. And it did the trick. The fire fizzled out.

"Thank you very much!" said Noah.

Then Noah gave Mrs Elephant and the monkeys – his Special Fire Brigade – a scrumptious tea.

24 A New Leaf

The billy kids had been very naughty. They had played butt and chase round Mrs Goat's washing line, and made the clean clothes dirty. They had left muddy footprints all over the carpet. And, as if that wasn't bad enough, they had knocked over a vase and smashed it.

Mrs Goat was not pleased.

"You had better turn over a new leaf," she said crossly, "or you'll both go to bed without any supper."

The billy kids ran outside to do *exactly* as Mrs Goat had told them.

"I wonder why we have to turn over a new leaf?" said the first billy kid.

"I don't know," said the other, "but we'd better do it quickly. I want my supper."

It was the time of year when the trees were bare. So no matter how hard they looked, the billy kids couldn't find a new leaf anywhere. There were some leaves on the ground but these were old and brown.

After a while Mrs Goat came out to see what they were doing. When they told her, she laughed.

"Silly billies," she said. "Turning over a new leaf means you have to behave well from now on."

The billy kids promised to be as good as they could, and they began by laying the table for supper.

25 Monster Skipping

The little monsters Meeny, Miny and Mo were watching some friends skipping. It looked fun.

"I wish we could skip," said Meeny.

"We haven't got a rope," said Miny and Mo.

At that very moment a Pongo worm popped out of a hole.

He was long and skinny - just like a rope. It gave Meeny an idea.

"Will you play skipping with us?" he asked.

The Pongo worm said he would. So two little monsters took turns holding each end, while one skipped in the middle. The worm was tickled pink. That's monster skipping for you.

But remember, if you want to skip like that - you'll have to go to Pongo!

26 Pumpkin Pie

Oh my! pumpkin pie.
Make them and bake them and
Pile 'em up high.

One for a daddy,
Two for a mummy,
Three for a baby with a fat pink tummy.
Four for the boys,
Five for the girls,
Six for the child with the long dark curls.
Seven for Jack,
Eight for Jill,
Nine for the scarecrow on the hill.
Ten for the farmer's jolly wife -
She's grown pumpkins all her life!

27 Where Would You Live?

Where would you live, if you could choose?
Where would you like to be?
Imagine your home was a castle of stone,
Or a shack on the shore, by the sea.

Perhaps you'd like a houseboat,
Or a caravan on wheels?
A home to move about in, to sleep and have your meals.

Maybe you'd choose a tree house,
Where branches brush the sky.
Or a rooftop flat in a city, to watch the clouds go by.

A cave underground might be cosy,
You could live there, curled up like a ball.
But I think the place where you live NOW -
Is the very best home of all!

28 Ten Grey Rabbits and One Sly Fox

10   Ten grey rabbits and one sly fox
20   Twenty new crayons in one long box
30   Thirty cups and saucers and one teapot
40   Forty balls of wool and one big knot!
50   Fifty buzzy bees and one jar of honey
60   Sixty silver coins and one bag of money
70   Seventy cheeky mice and one lazy cat
80   Eighty bouncing balls and one wooden bat
90   Ninety crawling crabs and one slippery rock
100   One hundred little keys for one big lock

243

29 Puff to the Rescue

Puff and Davy had been together for a long time. Puff was an old steam engine and Davy was his driver. All summer Puff pulled little carriages filled with holidaymakers up the mountain railway. The children loved him.

In winter nobody had much use for an old-fashioned steam train. People travelled to work by high-speed expresses. Puff was far too slow for them. But Davy kept Puff's paint and brasswork clean, and oiled his wheels every day.

One November night there was a terrible storm, and the wind blew fiercely round the mountain. Next morning Davy went to the engine shed as usual. Suddenly the Station Master ran in, looking very worried.

"What's the matter?" asked Davy.

"Emergency!" panted the Station Master. "The storm has blown a tree down across the track. It's smashed the signal box too."

"There's an express train due in an hour," said Davy. "There'll be a crash if we don't move it. Come on Puff, this is a job for you!"

Puff needed lots of coal and water to make him go. Davy shovelled lumps of coal into the firebox and filled the water tank. Soon there was a roaring fire inside Puff's boiler, and smoke was pouring out of his chimney. When the steam pressure was right, Davy pulled a lever inside the cab. There was a loud hiss and *SSSHOOOMPH!* as the steam rushed into the pistons and turned the wheels. Then with a *peep-peep!* from the whistle, they were off, chugging along the line.

Puff went as fast as he could with Davy at the controls. They were

coming round a bend, when Davy saw the tree blocking their way. Puff slowed down. Then he nudged forward *choo . . . choo . . . choo* and pushed the tree out of the way. Davy just had time to shunt Puff on to a side line, before the express came speeding by. *BEEEEE-BORE!* blared the hooter, and the driver gave a cheery wave.

Soon everyone got to hear about how Puff had saved the day. Then more and more visitors came to see the famous steam engine, so Puff and Davy were kept busy all the time. *Peep-peep!*

30 School Rules

One at a time
Keep in line,
Don't talk
Walk!
Don't run
Have fun but
Don't bully
Wear your woolly,
Shut the door
Sit on the floor and
Don't wriggle
Or giggle at prayers
Don't play on the stairs
Stop making that noise and . . .
BE GOOD GIRLS AND BOYS!

Open Up the Windows

Open up the windows
Peep behind each door
Every day 'til Christmas
One to twenty-four!

Christmas candles glowing bright
A jolly snowman, glistening white
Holly sprigs with round red berries
A party cake with nuts and cherries
Ivy and some mistletoe
Boots for walking in the snow
Sticks of candy in a jar
A super pedal racing car
A Christmas tree with twinkling lights
Logs to burn on winter nights
Silver bells that ring-a-ding-ding
Presents wrapped and tied with string
Tasty biscuits made with spice
Chocolate coated sugar mice
A goose and turkey, big and fat
Crackers and a paper hat
Carol singers at the gate
Hot plum pudding on a plate
A cottage made of gingerbread
Christmas stockings by the bed
Santa with his sack of toys
Dancing dolls and drummer boys
A shooting star to light the way . . .
For Santa and his reindeer sleigh.

2 A Special Job for Fergus

One morning early in December, Malcolm drove Fergus to the woods near the farm. He was towing a long trailer.

"We've got a special job to do today," he said.

The farmer steered Fergus along a wide track, with rows and rows of fir trees on either side. They stopped near a woodcutter cutting one with a chain saw. The whirring blade made a deafening noise as it sliced through the trunk. Bzzzzzzzzeeeeee! There was a pause then, SHOOOSH! The tree toppled over.

"You asked for a large Christmas tree," said the woodcutter. "Will this one do?"

"Thank you," said Malcolm. "It's just right. Let's load it up."

Fergus waited while the two men heaved the tree on to the trailer. Then Malcolm revved up the engine and Fergus moved slowly forward. The deep grooves on his tyres gripped the rough, muddy ground easily.

Once they were on the road again, Fergus went more quickly. They drove straight to the town hospital! A hospital porter was waiting to help Malcolm carry the tree inside. They stood it in a tub where everyone could see it, and draped the branches with decorations and coloured lights. As Malcolm switched them on, a nurse brought some patients from the Children's Ward to have a look.

"Ooo!" said all the children, gazing up at the glittering branches.

When it was time to go, everyone said goodbye and thanked Malcolm and Fergus for coming.

"Get well soon!" shouted Malcolm.

Then with a cheery hoot on the horn, he drove Fergus back to the farm.

247

3 China Tea

Said the little china dog
To the little china cat,
"Let's go fishing in a little china hat."
They caught a china fish
In a little china sea -
Put it on a china dish
And ate it up for tea.

4 An Important Letter

Dear Father Christmas,
Would you please
Bring me all or some of these;
A talking doll with lots of clothes
(I really would like one of those)
Some colouring pens,
A diamond ring -
Not of course the real thing!
A pocket torch,
A puzzle game,
A rocking horse with flying mane . . .
But there's one thing
I quite forgot,
We haven't got a chimney pot.
Can you find some other way
To bring me toys on Christmas Day?
I've tried my hardest to be good!
With lots of love from,
Emma Wood

5 December Days

December days, dark by teatime,
Holly berries on the bough,
Frosty patterns at the windows,
Winter winds blow colder now.

Silently, while we lie sleeping
Snowflakes settle through the night.
Flake on flake, these icy crystals
Turn our world to dazzling white.

6 All Sorts of Parcels

Newly-wrapped presents
All shapes and sizes;
Round, square, rectangle -
Full of surprises.
Star, cube and triangle
Under the tree.
I wonder which parcel
Was put there for ME?

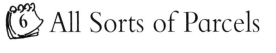

7 Noah's Baking Day

One day just before Christmas, Noah made a list of all the animals living in the Park. It was a long list! Then he drew a picture of each one on a piece of cardboard, and cut them out. He made cut-outs of Flip and Flap the penguins, Mrs Stegosaurus, Mr Robin Redbreast, Mrs Elephant, the monkeys . . . animals of all shapes and sizes.

"Now for some fun!" said Noah, putting on his apron and opening a cookery book. "Let me see . . . I need butter, flour, eggs and sugar."

He mixed the ingredients together in a large mixing bowl, to make biscuit dough, and rolled it out with a rolling pin.

"I need my special cutters next," he said.

Noah greased one side of each cardboard cut-out, and placed it on the rolled-out dough. Then he cut round each one with a knife. When all the animal shapes had been cut out, Noah mixed up some egg yolk, water and food colouring, and painted the biscuits with a little paintbrush. To finish them off, he used currants and cherries to make eyes and noses.

"Phew!" said Noah. "Nearly done."

Carefully he lifted each biscuit on to a baking tray, and put them in a hot oven to cook. When they were done, he took them out and left them to cool.

Later, Noah tied the biscuits with thread, and hung them on his Christmas tree - special presents, one for every animal in the Park!

fairy lights

8 Birthday Post

Early in the morning down our street
The postman comes on his two flat feet.
He stops at Number Forty-Four
And rat-a-tat-tat! knocks on our door.
Postman! Postman! let me see
How many birthday cards for me?
Ten, eleven, twelve or more . . .
Higgeldy-piggeldy on the floor!

9 Good Mother Hubbard

Good Mother Hubbard
Lives in a cupboard,
Up on the very top shelf;
With a nice friendly spider
Who sits right beside her,
She weaves all the cobwebs herself!

10 Abigail's Pony

Abigail's pony, once found he was able
To open the door and trot out of the stable.
He rolled in the mud with his best rug on,
Then went to the barn and ate too much corn.
He lost a shoe when he jumped the gate,
And didn't get home 'til half-past-eight!

11 All I Have is a Violin

All I have is a violin,
With a crooked bow and a broken string.
But I can sing and I can play
To chase the moodiest blues away.
Skip to the East,
Hop to the West,
Dance with a friend that you like best!

250

12 Snow Trouble!

In wintertime Doctor Dog and Nurse Kitty are busier than ever. They have lots of sick patients to call on. Rush, rush, rush!

But today it has been snowing and Doctor Dog has to drive slowly on the icy road. Suddenly a van comes speeding round a corner. It is being chased by Police Constable Fox in his police car. He is trying to catch some bank robbers.

"Look out!" says Doctor Dog, swerving to avoid an accident. His car skids into a snowdrift.

"Help!" says Nurse Kitty.

Police Constable Fox stops to make sure Doctor Dog and Nurse Kitty are all right. They are not hurt but their car is stuck in the snow.

"I could tow you out with my car," says Police Constable Fox, "but I haven't got a rope."

Nurse Kitty opens her First Aid box.

"Try this," she says, handing the policeman a roll of bandage.

Police Constable Fox ties one end to the back of his car, and the other end to Doctor Dog's bumper. Nurse Kitty's tow-rope works perfectly, and the doctor's car is out of trouble in no time.

"Goodbye," says Police Constable Fox, as Doctor Dog and Nurse Kitty drive off to visit their patients.

"Now I must go after those bank robbers."

Drive carefully Police Constable Fox. There's been enough trouble for one day!

13 Spare a Thought

Spare a thought,
Give some crumbs
To the birds when winter comes.
Feed them well
And you will hear
Chirpy, "Thank you's!" through the year.

🗓14 Magic Gifts

Once upon a time there was a beautiful princess called Makeda. But one day she fell ill. No doctor could cure her. The king was very sad. He said he would give a fortune to anyone who could make his daughter well again.

Now a shoemaker lived near the palace. He had barely enough money to feed his wife and son, let alone buy leather to make shoes. Soon he had only two pairs left to sell.

"Take them to market," he told his son, Simon. "Get the best price you can. We'll use the money to buy some food."

So Simon set off and on the way he passed the palace. He wanted to catch a glimpse of the princess. He had often seen her walking in the garden. Little did he know how ill she was.

When he reached the market, the first person he met was a strange-looking woman. She eyed the shoes enviously because her own had holes in them. Then she held out a small green apple.

"Those are fine shoes," said the woman. "Will you swop them for this special apple?"

"What's so special about it?" asked Simon. "It looks sour to me."

"It's magic," said the woman. "It will make a sick person well."

Simon agreed, but when she had gone he said to himself,

"What a silly thing to do! I must sell this last pair of shoes for lots of money, or we'll have nothing to eat."

Just then a musician came by. He had no shoes at all. He stopped to play Simon a tune on his flute.

"Those are fine shoes," said the musician, peering at them through a pair of spectacles. "Will you swop them for these special glasses?"

"What's so special about them?" asked Simon.

"They're magic," said the musician. "They'll show you the girl you are to marry and take you to her side."

"I should like that!" said Simon, forgetting all about the money. He gave the musician the shoes and put the glasses ON.

No sooner were they on than, to his astonishment, he saw Princess Makeda, lying ill at the palace. And in two blinks he was at her side. The princess looked tired and thin but Simon fell in love with her at once. She thought Simon was the most handsome man she had ever seen, and loved him too.

Simon gave her the magic apple and sure enough, after the very first bite, the princess began to feel better. By the time she had nibbled it down to the core, she was up and dancing round the room.

The king gave Simon more gold than he could imagine and his family were never hungry again. Prince Simon married Princess Makeda and they all lived happily ever after.

The School Play

I'm in the school play this Christmas,
I've got an important part;
So I'm learning and learning and learning my lines
Until I can say them by heart.

When I go on stage I'll be nervous,
I'm sure I'll forget what to say.
You see I'm the front of the pantomime horse -
"Neigh, neigh, neigh, neigh, NEIGH!"

16 The Good Fairy

Lucy came running in from school one day. Mrs MacGee was making the children's tea.

"I'm going to be in the school play!" said Lucy.

"What as?" asked Mrs MacGee.

"The Good Fairy," said Lucy.

"Huh!" said her brother, Neil. "Is that all."

Lucy took no notice of him. She learnt her lines and Mrs MacGee made a costume. The wings were spectacular! But at the dress rehearsal, everything went wrong.

"I'll never get it right," cried Lucy at bedtime.

"A bad rehearsal often means a good performance," said Mrs MacGee. "You mark my words."

On the first night of the school play Lucy was nervous. Her legs felt like jelly, as she waited at the side of the stage. Everyone in her class was acting their parts brilliantly. She was sure she would ruin the play. At last it was time for her to go on.

"Good luck!" whispered Lucy's teacher, giving her a gentle push.

Lucy twirled on to the stage. Her wings slipped a bit, but she said her lines perfectly. And, with a flick of her wand, she turned the wicked witch into a frog.

At the end of the play, the audience clapped and cheered. Lucy could just see Mrs MacGee and Neil sitting in the front row. They were cheering the loudest of all.

"You were great," said Neil, after the show.

"A super-duper star!" said Mrs MacGee.

And she took the children home.

17 Jobs for Potter Pig

Potter Pig was counting the money in his piggy bank. He wanted to buy birthday presents for the piglets, but he hadn't saved quite enough.

"You could earn some extra pocket money," said Mrs Pig. "I have one or two jobs you could do."

First, Potter helped by doing the washing up. He squirted too much washing-up liquid into the water. There were bubbles everywhere.

"Never mind," said Mrs Pig, mopping up the mess. "You've got the dishes nice and clean."

Next Potter went to the shops and fetched some groceries. He carried home two heavy bags of shopping.

"Well done," said Mrs Pig. "You are a great help."

Just then Mr Pig came in.

"I've got a job for you, Potter," he said. "You can clean the car."

So Potter spent all afternoon doing that. By teatime he was very tired, but he had earned a lot of pocket money.

"Now I can buy birthday presents," said Potter happily, "and some sweets for myself!"

18 Tree Fairy

Christmas fairy on the tree
Although you look so pretty,
You're stuck up there
While we're down here –
Now, isn't that a pity!

255

19 Mrs Jolly's Wrapping Robot

Mrs Jolly's toyshop is the best in town. At Christmastime it is full of people buying toys, and everyone wants them gift-wrapped. Trains, puppets, trucks and dolls - Mrs Jolly wraps them all. Each parcel takes quite a time.

So this year Mrs Jolly decided to speed things up. She invented a wrapping robot! It was a machine with rolls of brightly coloured paper at one end, and spools of ribbon at the other. In the middle were boxes of all shapes and sizes.

At first Mrs Jolly had a few problems with her new invention. She put a box of play-bricks in the machine and switched it on. The robot picked the bricks up with its metal arms, and threw them all over the place.

Another time, the lever which unwound the wrapping paper got stuck in the 'ON' position, so the robot wrapped one teddy bear sixteen times!

Mrs Jolly adjusted a few knobs and got everything working properly. From then on the robot wrapped, tucked, folded and tied each parcel perfectly.

It saved a lot of time. The robot wrapped twelve presents a minute!

More and more people came to Mrs Jolly's toyshop, and she was busier than ever.

"What a wonderful wrapping robot!" said her customers.

"Thank you," said Mrs Jolly. "And A Very Merry Christmas to you all!"

20 Snowmen Now and Then

Long ago
Believe it or not
Snowmen lived where it's always hot!

They didn't drip
Or melt away
But played and swam at the beach all day.

Things have changed
Now, you know,
Snowmen love the cold and snow.

If you see one
Down your street,
Don't try to warm his hands and feet!

21 Little Angel

"Be a little angel,"
My Daddy said to me.
"Help me with these lights and bells,
To decorate our tree."

"Be a little angel,"
At bedtime Mummy said.
"Wash your face and clean your teeth,
Then quickly into bed."

I'm hoping Father Christmas
Will know that I've been good.
All day I've done as I've been told –
As little angels should!

22 Lottie's Goat

Lottie bought a billy goat
And Butter was his name.
He biffed and butted anyone
If they too near him came.
Said Lottie, "If you don't behave
I'll send you back again!"

23 Give and Take

You throw,
I catch,
Some give,
Others snatch.
I lend,
You borrow,
Yours today,
Mine tomorrow.

24 Father Christmas and the Saucy Pirates

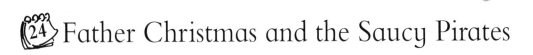

It was Christmas Eve. Captain Scuttlebutt and the Saucy Pirates were going to the North Pole, where Father Christmas lived.

"It's not fair!" said Snitch and Snatch. "Father Christmas never brings us any presents."

"That's because we're pirates," said Maggot, the cook.

"Well, me hearties," said Captain Scuttlebutt, "we'll kidnap him tonight. Then he'll have to fill our stockings!"

The Saucy Pirates moored their ship, *The Bag o' Bones* behind an iceberg. They planned to lure Father Christmas there with a trick.

First Snitch and Snatch left a trail of carrots in the snow. Then Maggot made some mince pies and left them to cool on deck. Captain Scuttlebutt looked through his telescope. He could see Father Christmas in his sleigh with the reindeer, ready to fly.

"Off we go," cried Father Christmas.

But the reindeer had spotted the carrots. They followed the trail, munching happily. The pirates' plan was working! When the sleigh reached the *The Bag o' Bones*, Father Christmas sniffed. He could smell the mince pies. "Mmmm!" he sighed.

"Got you!" yelled Captain Scuttlebutt, bundling him aboard.

"Give us some presents," said Snitch and Snatch.

"No," said Father Christmas. "You've been very naughty pirates."

Luckily Sam and Wallace came chugging along in *The Topsy Turvy*. They had been fishing and were on their way home.

"Let Father Christmas go at once," said Sam.

The pirates said they were sorry and promised to be good. Then Maggot gave Father Christmas a plateful of mince pies.

"Delicious!" he said. "Now I must be on my way."

But later that night, when the pirates were fast asleep, Father Christmas came back and filled their stockings. After all, they said they were going to be good, didn't they?

When Sam woke up next morning, he found lots of presents in his stocking, with a 'Thank You' note from Father Christmas. And there was an extra large kipper for Wallace!

25 One Bright Star

One bright star,
Three wise men,
Taking gifts to Bethlehem.

One bright star
Points the way
To one little King on Christmas Day.

26 Little Bear in the Snow

Little Bear looks out of his window one morning. It has been snowing! There is thick white snow everywhere.

"Ooo!" says Little Bear. "Can I go out?"

"Yes," says Mrs Bear. "But wrap up warm."

First Little Bear puts on his snowsuit and zips up the long red zipper. Then he puts on his great big boots, his furry ear-muffs, and the woolly mittens Grandma knitted him. He is all wrapped up like a parcel.

Little Bear looks at himself in the mirror and laughs.

"I can't move!" he says.

Just then there is a rat-a-tat-tat at the door. Little Bear's friends have called round to see him. They have brought a sledge.

"Off you go," says Mrs Bear.

And crunch, crunch, crunch! Little Bear goes out in the snow to play.

27 Ben's Birthday Surprise

Ben's birthday was just after Christmas. This year he wasn't having a party - his nan had planned a surprise.

"Choose three friends," she had told him. "I'm taking you out for a treat."

On the morning of his birthday Ben was very excited. The postman brought him lots of cards, and he opened some presents from Mum and Dad. His friends, Joshua, Catherine and Kim arrived. Finally he heard a toot-toot! outside, and there was Nan, waiting in the car. Ben ran and gave her a hug.

"Where are we going?" he asked as they all climbed in.

"Aha!" said Nan. "Wait and see."

She drove down the motorway to a big town, and parked the car near a square. Then she hurried the children across the square to . . . a theatre!

"Oh, Nan," cried Ben. "Are we going to a pantomime? Look. It's Jack and the Beanstalk."

"I've got tickets for the very best seats," she said.

Ben and his friends had a wonderful time. The giant was really big and scary. After the show they went for a special tea at the Theatre Café. The waitress brought them a cake with candles and Happy Birthday Ben in icing on the top.

When they got home Ben kissed his nan goodbye.

"Thank you," he said. "That was the best birthday ever!"

28 Katie's Good Turn

Ma and Katie were visiting Granny Purrkins in hospital. Katie had made a get-well card, and Ma had brought some flowers. Granny Purrkins was very pleased to see them, but she looked worried.

"Who will water my plants while I'm here?" she said.

"I will," said Katie.

When they got home Ma found a special watering can which had a long spout. Katie went round to her Granny's house every day and watered the plants. There were pots and pots of them in the kitchen, and some that trailed all the way down the stairs.

But Katie's favourite was a hyacinth. She could just see the tip of a bud at the top of its stem. I wonder what colour the flowers will be? she thought.

On the day Granny Purrkins came home from hospital, the hyacinth burst into bright pink flowers. Katie thought it was beautiful.

"Thank you for looking after ALL my plants," said Granny. And she gave Katie the hyacinth. "Now you have one of your own!"

29 Winter Roadworks

Holes to fill! Holes to fill!
Here is the man with a noisy drill.

Mind the load! Mind the load!
This truck has stones to mend the road.

Heat the tar! Heat the tar!
Then roll it flat as a chocolate bar.

Clear the way! Clear the way!
For all the lorries and cars today.

30 Mr Marzipan's Magic Wand

Mr Marzipan was a bit of a wizard. He could make things larger or smaller, just by tapping them with his magic wand. One end made things grow, the other made them shrink.

But one day, while he was out shopping, the wizard dropped his wand. A little puppy called Fudge happened to see it, and picked it up. Fudge thought it was a stick to play with! The puppy ran along the pavement with one end sticking out of his mouth.

Tap-tap-tap! Mr Marzipan's wand knocked against the shops in the High Street. The shops shrank to the size of dolls' houses.

Then Fudge trotted off to the park. Tap-tap-tap! went the wand, as the other end brushed against some trees. The trees grew enormous. So did the birds sitting in the branches. They were as big as aeroplanes!

It didn't take long for Mr Marzipan to discover what had happened. The wizard soon spotted Fudge amongst the giant trees.

"Please give me my wand," he said. "I'll give you a reward for finding it."

Fudge dropped the wand, and Mr Marzipan changed everything back to its proper size. Then the wizard took the puppy to the butcher's shop, to buy him a large bone.

"I've only got a small one left, I'm afraid," said the butcher.

Well, I expect you can guess what happened next, can't you? That's right. Tap-tap-tap! Mr Marzipan turned that little bone into the biggest one ever. Fudge took all week to finish it!

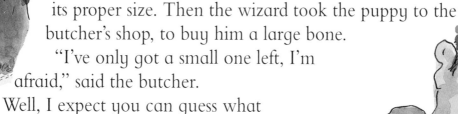

A Year Full of Days

365 days make one whole year,
But once in every four
366 days make a Leap Year -
That year has one day more.

There are 7 days in every week
For work and play and rest,
But the day I wait a year for . . .
Is MY BIRTHDAY - that's the best!